ANCHORS
for HOPE

Trusting God's Security Through the Storm of Childhood Cancer

BY KAREN F. FURR

ANCHORSFORHOPE.COM

Table of Contents

Free Gift	4
Praise	5
Acknowledgements	7
Chapter 1	9
Chapter 2	13
Chapter 3	17
Chapter 4	25
Chapter 5	31
Chapter 6	37
Chapter 7	41
Chapter 8	49
Chapter 9	55
Chapter 10	63
Chapter 11	71
Chapter 12	77
Chapter 13	81
Chapter 14	85
Chapter 15	89
Chapter 16	97
Chapter 17	101
Chapter 18	109
Chapter 19	113
Chapter 20	121
Chapter 21	125
Afterward	133
About the Author	139
Videos of Lauren's cancer journey	140
Websites of childhood cancer	141
Credits	142

Thank you for buying my book!

I'd like to offer you a FREE GIFT:

15 Practical Ways to Help a Family In Need (Besides a Casserole!)

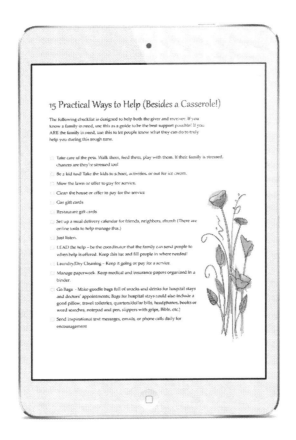

Grab your copy FREE at
AnchorsForHope.com/FreeGift

PRAISE FOR LAUREN'S JOURNEY AND FOR THIS BOOK,

Anchors For Hope: Trusting God's Security Through the Storm of Childhood Cancer

Seeing Lauren's strength and her trust in God through this whole journey blessed our family and showed us that even in the midst of darkness we are called to be steadfast in trusting in what God is doing, rather than to lose our faith. I think it united all of us that were following her journey, whether near or far, and showed us all the power of prayer first in her little victories, and then ultimately in one great big final victory over cancer.
—*Mike and Nicki Landers*

[Karen's] constant positivity and Lauren's sweet spirit even through the toughest moments were so encouraging and uplifting. And what rejoicing when the "all clears" started coming in! It really taught me that no matter how daunting our reality that we face, God is bigger. Which means I can certainly trust Him with the much smaller day to day challenges! If God can heal precious little Lauren, He can do anything. And if Lauren can stay focused and positive in the midst, I certainly can as well! Thank you all for being an example to the rest of us when our futures seem uncertain and scary. God is bigger! God is greater!
—*Kimberly Sizemore*

Lauren's journey showed me how a family can be united and not divided during such a difficult time. God's love poured out from this family and God got all the glory.
—*Amy Robbins*

Lauren showed me that no matter how huge the obstacles are in life, our hope is truly in the Lord.
—*Steve Maples*

Lauren's journey reminded me that God is bigger than the darkest scariest times in our lives. She's showed me bravery, faith, courage, and strength! She's my hero!
—*Jana Strickland*

God showed me through Lauren to not take life for granted. Truly love one another to include your enemy and having faith the size of a mustard seed, you will be able to move mountains!
—*Mike Sabens*

Watching the journey, God never left. When the days were unending, faith carried you through. When good results came, God was given praise. The journey displayed that no matter what the circumstance, God's love is ever present- beautiful story!
—*Jean Fortgang*

ACKNOWLEDGEMENTS

How can I even begin to thank all of the people who have supported and loved us through this journey? The list would go on for pages, and that would only include the people I know. There were so many anonymous givers and prayer warriors all over the world. I am thankful for every single person who gave, prayed, or even spent a moment in thought for our family. Of course, I am most thankful to God. His provisions are abundant.

Brian, Audrey, Haley, and Lauren—thank you for being strong and staying committed to our family during this journey. We were all effected in different ways, but each of you contributed your strengths to this family and made us the best "whole" we could be.

Morgan, thank you for being my encourager, my mentor and teacher, and mostly my friend. This book would probably have never happened without your guidance. But you have done so much more than work through a book with me. You've helped me heal emotionally and helped me find my voice in this journey. I'm so glad God brought you into this journey, too!

Finally, to my readers! Thank you for giving your time to read this book! My sincere prayer is that somewhere in our story you will find hope and inspiration. My greatest desire is that God will be glorified and that you will know Him better because of your time spent with me.

CHAPTER 1

"She is more precious than rubies; nothing you desire can compare with her." Proverbs 3:15 NIV.

Lauren was my second child. She came into the world during a crazy time in my life. I was already a single mom to a beautiful baby girl, Audrey, who was only a year and a half when Lauren was born. We relied on food stamps and my part time job just to provide the basics. I was scared, ashamed, and insecure. I was drudging my way through nursing school in hopes of providing a solid foundation for me and my girls, and I was living in my parents' basement at the time. Just when I thought I couldn't handle anything else, on March 29, 2004 God gave me the sweetest, most precious baby. She slept through the night, ate well, and rarely cried. She was easy going and laid back—a dream baby, really.

Hurricane Katrina hit Louisiana in August 2005, when Lauren was 17 months old. The girls and I were safe, since we were living with my parents in Tennessee, but my dad did some special work with Federal Emergency Management Agency at the time and had to go into New Orleans to help with clean up and recovery. He spent three weeks helping with disaster relief. The girls missed him terribly because he had become a father figure to them. When he came home, Audrey and Lauren were ecstatic. They screamed his name, climbed on his back, and gave him a thousand kisses! "Pappaw's home, pick me up Pappaw, kiss me Pappaw!" As excited as they were to see him, though, they kept peeking in his bags to see what presents he'd brought back for them.

I only remember one thing he brought back. He pulled a simple string of Mardi Gras beads from his suitcase and handed them to Lauren. My sweet, quiet baby girl smiled like never before when she saw those beads. They were special! She immediately pulled off her shirt, yanked off her pants, completely stripped down to her diaper, and tore down her ponytail. I watched with anticipation and confusion, I'd never seen her this excited before! Then, with great confidence, she put on those beads, puffed out her chest, and posed for the camera. I promise you, that moment was life changing somehow! It was a moment none of us will ever forget. Even to this day, when Lauren says something sassy or gets out of line, we laugh and say, "It's those Mardi Gras beads!" The picture from that moment still hangs on our fridge! We had no idea at the time how impactful that moment would be.

From that day on, Lauren became a rebel to the core. If there were trouble, she would find it. I can't count the number of days we dragged Lauren, kicking and screaming into preschool. I didn't even know this was possible until it actually happened, but at the age of four, she was kicked out of Sunday School! I just knew I had failed as a parent. I read every parenting book and tried every approach —rewarding good behavior, punishing bad behavior, time out, sticker charts, spanking—you name it, and I tried it. I even took her up to the altar at church one Sunday morning and prayed over her because I thought she might be possessed!

Chapter 1

Around that same time, Lauren also stopped growing at a "normal" rate. Her height and weight measurements were so far behind her peers that her pediatrician ordered some tests, which were all normal. Everyone in my family is short, so we just assumed she got my genes. But, her size was becoming an everyday problem for her. Because she looked younger than she was, people treated her that way. And pretty soon, she began to act the way she was treated. She was picked on quite a bit in preschool and kindergarten, so we focused on building self-esteem and confidence at home.

By first grade, we started seeing a shift, and by second grade all of our "teaching" kicked in, and her confidence and ego went into overdrive. Lauren became the bully. I'll never forget the day I received a call from the assistant principal that Lauren was going to be expelled if there were any more incidents of bullying—*in second grade!* I was eating lunch in the break room at work when I got this call, and when I hung up I went crying into my boss's office, at my whit's end with no idea what to do. When I spoke to the principal, she reassured me that I was doing the right things as a parent and that we were in a partnership to help Lauren succeed. She smiled and said, "There is a reason God gave that girl such a spunky, fighting spirit. We just have to figure out why, and teach her to use it for good." Little did I know how prophetic those words would be.

Third and fourth grade were transitional for Lauren. With amazing teachers, she started to really balance self-confidence with respect and began to excel. She even made a perfect score on her state math test in third grade! We felt like we were finally on the right track and that the rough patch was over. Time to move forward, or so we thought.

*Lauren at Christmastime, age nine
(three months prior to diagnosis)*

CHAPTER 2

"For I know the plans I have for you," declares the Lord, "plans to prosper you and not to harm you, plans to give you hope and a future" Jeremiah 29:11 NIV.

It's kind of funny how chaotic life can seem when you're busy living it, but when you look back, the path you've traveled seems so perfectly aligned. Despite my bad decisions and seemingly uncoordinated launch into adulthood, I truly believe now that God was preparing me for being the mother that Lauren would need. After graduating high school, I went to college with several career options in mind. I was interested in foreign missions, business, and healthcare, but most of all I wanted to be an English major.

I loved to read, write, and touch books. Walking through a book store is like heaven to me. I daydreamed about becoming a book editor—a job where I could read books all day long, edit them, and help make them better. But when I found myself as a young mother, facing divorce and another baby on the way, it was time to make a decision. My dad, who is my mentor and hero, said to me, "You can't choose if you get through this, but you can choose how you get through it." So I decided to follow in my mom's footsteps and become a nurse, knowing that a career as a nurse would be a stable career path with which I could financially support myself and my babies. I wasn't really passionate about the career, but it didn't totally bore me, so I decided to go with it.

During nursing school, I had the privilege of working as a secretary for the nursing executives at East Tennessee Children's Hospital in Knoxville, Tennessee. I would come in during the evenings, type up meeting minutes and policies, and do an assortment of copying, printing, and sorting tasks. Being in that office, I learned so much about how a hospital, particularly a pediatric hospital, worked behind the scenes. I also learned about all of the different departments that made up the whole of the institution. One night, as I was nearing graduation, the manager of the Pediatric Intensive Care Unit (PICU) came in to get his mail. He stopped to chat and asked if I had a job yet. I told him that I did not, and he replied, "Want to come work for me?" I said yes, and that was it, I had my first nursing job. I had never really thought about what direction I wanted to go in nursing, or even about setting up interviews, but God knew exactly where He wanted me, and He laid it in my lap.

Working in the PICU was exhilarating, challenging, and emotionally draining. To see children at their sickest, parents at their weakest, and doctors and nurses at their finest is an amazing experience. Whenever people would say to me, "I don't know how you do what you do," my response would always be, "I love working with sick kids because they don't care that they're sick. They are still so full of hope and joy." The most inspiring part of working with children is that they always want to ride a tricycle or play a game, regardless of their circumstances. Even for the sickest little ones, they don't understand what they might not get to experience in life, so they don't know to be depressed about it. They simply live life one precious day at a time.

Chapter 2

About two months before I graduated from nursing school, I met an amazing man named Brian, who had a daughter the same age as my Audrey. After two years of dating, we got married, formed a new family of five, and settled in Atlanta, Georgia. I began working in the PICU at Children's Healthcare of Atlanta at Scottish Rite. The patients under my charge in Atlanta had much more intense illnesses and issues than what I had faced in Tennessee, and the mental toughness required to do the job was extreme. I took care of kids with heart problems, lung problems, injuries from car accidents and accidents with lawnmowers, pit bull attacks, child abuse, and many other horrible things. The worst for me were the kids with infections or trauma, because I always thought, "This could be my own child."

I worked as a PICU nurse for five years before I decided I needed to take a break. I had reached my limit. I would go home and close my eyes and see my own children in beds at the PICU, hooked up to breathing tubes and IVs.

I transferred to a different department and worked for about a year in the Pediatric Cardiac Catheterization Lab, after which I took a job with a medical consulting company where I learned about all of the ins and outs of Medicaid programs and services. This led to an opportunity to work from home, and provided me more availability to be with my own children. I didn't see it then, but God had prepared my career path to align with the knowledge and support I needed to be Lauren's caregiver and still provide for my family.

CHAPTER 3

"Out of the south comes the storm, And out of the north the cold." Job 37:9 NASB

In March of 2014, all the kids at our neighborhood bus stop came down with a stomach bug. Lauren was the first in our household to get sick. I knew it was only a matter of time before the other girls got sick too. Since Lauren was already feeling better by the weekend, and Audrey and Haley were just starting to deal with the bug, Brian and Lauren decided to spend Saturday night on our boat at the lake. I spoke to Brian on the phone on Sunday morning, and he told me they had a great time. He said Lauren had a little bit of a headache, probably from motion sickness because it was windy and the lake was a little rough. They were going to stop for breakfast at McDonalds before heading to church. Just a normal Sunday morning.

I settled in with my coffee and Bible on the couch while Audrey and Haley slept. About 30 minutes later, Brian called and said that Lauren threw up in the church hallway. There he was, trying to get ready to teach his fourth grade Sunday School class, and she pukes right in the carpeted hallway. He cleaned up the best he could, let the director know, and then they came home. She joined the sleeping bunch upstairs, and Brian and I spent the rest of the day serving Gatorade and saltines.

On Monday morning Haley was feeling better, so she went to school. Audrey was still not feeling great, so Brian stayed home from work with her. I took Lauren to the pediatrician to make sure nothing else was going on since her illness had lingered, and they said to call back if she wasn't any better by Tuesday. The nurse practitioner reassured me that there were multiple stomach bugs going around and Lauren had just been the "lucky" one to get hit twice. Tuesday morning came and Lauren was still complaining of nausea and a headache, so the pediatrician thought that she was probably just dehydrated from the stomach bugs and told us to take her to the local children's hospital emergency room for IV rehydration. Lauren had a tendency to be dramatic and take full advantage of any illness. She asked if she could stay in her pajamas, but Brian told her to get dressed for the day, wash her face, brush her teeth, and get ready. Who knew that that small decision would be such a big one in our memory for years to come? The things you do when you have no clue a tumor is growing in your baby's brain.

I called my manager to fill her in, kissed Brian goodbye, and told him I'd be back in a few hours. I remember sitting in the small hospital room in the emergency department with Lauren on March 11, 2014. As soon as the doctor came in the room, I felt we had a connection. Since I'd worked at the hospital several years before as an intensive care nurse, the doctor and I recognized each other from previous encounters, but there was something more powerful, more intuitive in our connection that day. I was comforted to know that Lauren was in good hands. Concurring with our thoughts of dehydration, she ordered some IV fluids for Lauren. However, even after the fluids, Lauren's headache wasn't subsiding. The doctor felt fairly

Chapter 3

certain then that we were dealing with migraines, but she must have had a divine nudge. I'll never forget her words.

"I really think she's suffering from migraines," she told me. "The best thing to do is follow up with a neurologist to determine the triggers and best treatment course for her. But, since you and I are both medical professionals and moms, I know we will both go to sleep wondering 'what if,' so I was thinking we could run a CT scan, just as a precaution, since you're already here and it will only take a few minutes."

I was happy to have the extra comfort from what I knew would be normal CT results, so I agreed. She gave me the required blurb of "Overexposure to radiation can increase risk of cancer . . ." but in my mind all I heard was "blah blah blah." I mean, what were the chances of my kid getting cancer? But when the doctor walked back into our room only minutes after the CT was done, I knew something was wrong.

The CT scan showed a tumor the size of a golf ball and some bleeding on Lauren's brain behind her right eye. The kind of tumor couldn't be determined by CT, but it was concerning for sure. The doctor told me she had already alerted the neurosurgeon on call and he would be arriving within the hour. She said he would probably want an MRI later that night and surgery in the morning. I wondered for just a moment which surgeon would be on call that day, but didn't take the time to ask. In less than two hours, we had gone from dehydration because of a stomach bug to planning surgery to remove a mass in my baby's brain. Whoever he was, I needed him desperately.

From the moment we received the CT scan results, our life of smooth sailing was blindsided by a hurricane of raging seas and high-speed winds. I called Brian first, trying to act calm and

19

reassuring so he wouldn't worry. He and Audrey had just pulled into the parking lot at Lowe's. I don't know why I remember that, but so many small details from that day are permanent in our minds, like snapshots. I told him that Lauren had had a CT scan and it showed a mass in her brain, that we weren't sure what it was, and that we needed to do some more tests. I asked him to take care of dinner for the other girls that evening and promised that I'd keep him posted. Since he'd lost his mom to a sudden illness several years before, I knew any uncertainty in my voice would terrify him, and I didn't want to do that until I knew what we were dealing with. All we knew so far was that there was a "tumor," but my mind had immediately wandered to the scary possibility of the "C" word—cancer.

I also called Lauren's dad, who lived in Tennessee, with the same approach. I thought if I could fake being calm long enough, I'd have time to figure it all out before panic set in. I told Lauren's dad not to make the four-hour drive to Atlanta until we had more information, and that I'd keep him informed of every detail as it came.

Once those phone calls were made, my brain went into nurse mode. I blocked out all emotions and started focusing on what to do and what facts I knew. This practice of separating emotion from facts, nurse-brain from mom-brain, would become one of my best strategies to manage anxiety and stress. Thankfully, Lauren was sleeping so she was not aware of what was happening or the panic that I'm sure my face would have revealed. We had a new puppy at home and an anniversary trip to Disney planned for the weekend. This was just a bad dream and I was going to wake up. There was no way that my baby had cancer.

When I had worked as a PICU nurse, I had worked with many severely ill children, but I rarely worked with cancer patients. I didn't specifically try to avoid them, but I just didn't encounter them often. The cancer patients always seemed to be assigned to other nurses, and I just helped out occasionally. Looking back, I don't doubt that God was protecting me from those patients, protecting me from becoming emotionally attached to their journeys, many of which ended tragically.

I do remember one very specific little girl I took care of who had been kicked in the head by a horse. I don't remember her so much because of her injury, but rather because of the neurosurgeon on her case. His incredible skill as a surgeon saved her life, and his genuine care for her as a child and for her parents was remarkably tender. I know now that God marked that memory in my mind as a future comfort. He knew that very same neurosurgeon would walk into Lauren's room that day in the ER and promise to take my daughter to surgery to save her life. I had worked with him many times as a PICU nurse, and he was exactly the surgeon I would have chosen if I could have. I believe, with my whole heart, that God prepared the staff that day for Lauren. Relief from his presence helped me hold off the panic a little longer.

When he entered the room, he gave me a hug and said, "I'll take great care of her." I knew he would, just as I had watched him take care of so many other kids before. He said he was very concerned about what he saw on the CT scan, and he wanted Lauren to have a detailed MRI later that evening. He had already cleared his schedule for the next day and planned to have her in surgery by 6:00 AM to remove the tumor.

The minute he left the room, I called Brian back and asked him to bring the girls to the hospital because we needed to be together as a family. I knew all too well that, depending on how surgery went, this could be the last time we would have the opportunity. I knew that we had the best surgeon and the best hospital at our fingertips, but I also knew that the look on that surgeon's face when he was explaining the plan was one of worry. I called Lauren's dad again and updated him on the surgeon's plan. He immediately headed to Atlanta. None of us knew what was going to happen, but we were all very aware of how fragile the situation was.

While we were waiting for an overnight hospital room, several of my friends who still worked in the PICU came down to visit in the ER room. Word had traveled fast, and every time another nurse, doctor, or staff member entered our room, I remembered the person from when I worked at the hospital. From the ER, through CT and MRI, onto the neurology floor, into surgery, through the recovery room, and into the PICU, Lauren was never in the hands of someone I hadn't worked with during my time there. Looking back, I can see how God had prepared the schedule of hospital staff in all departments for those days. She was never in the hands of a stranger, and God knew that was exactly what I would need to keep from falling apart in that first 24 hours.

Lauren's surgery went very well. The neurosurgeon said he was able to easily remove the entire tumor and felt good about the location and minimal damage. However, he did feel confident that the tumor was cancerous, and that revelation was a devastating blow to us. Once Lauren was settled in her PICU room, we were allowed to see her. When the PICU doctor came in to check on her, Lauren said, "Can you please decorate my room? Because it is ugly in here!" The nurse laughed and brought her some paints and paper. I remember thinking, "That's my girl!" That sassy, bossy, crafty girl was still there. I hadn't lost her. When Lauren asked for some brownies, someone brought her some Little Debbie Cosmic Brownies, and she ate the entire box. Later that night, she texted with one of her good friends, and sent a picture of her bandaged head and black eye. She was in such good spirits, completely unafraid of what had just happened or what was to come. To this day, she says that brain surgery was the easiest part of her cancer journey.

After spending one night in the PICU, Lauren's neurosurgeon felt that she was stable enough to move out of the PICU and into the regular neurology unit. Thanks to family and friends, this room was well-decorated before she got there. We wheeled Lauren into her room, and it was filled with flowers, sparkles, feather boas, and stuffed animals. Lauren had requested biscuits from Cracker Barrel, and when she opened the box to get one there was glitter inside. I had never felt so loved and cared for, and Lauren was smiling like she was at a party instead of in a hospital room.

Later that night, Lauren was acting particularly silly, giggling and playing with her toys. I asked her why she was acting that way and she said, "Mommy, I'm trying to be all smiles, because I don't want people to come see me and feel frowny. I want to make them all smiley!" No matter who came in her room or why, they did not leave without a smile on their face. She recovered beautifully from surgery and was able to go home the next day. Yes, within 72 hours she had gone to the hospital for a headache and nausea, had major brain surgery, been diagnosed with cancer, and gone home.

On Saturday we went shopping for some new, comfy clothes, and the following Saturday she played in her piano recital. That stubborn spunk that we had struggled to understand for years was starting to show its positive power.

After brain surgery, Lauren was prescribed a steroid that had to be taken several times a day, including one dose around midnight. This medicine made her so talkative that from about midnight to one in the morning for the first week after surgery, we would have nightly "chats," with her chatting and me trying to stay awake. One night she told me an elaborate storyline of movies she wanted to create with the hero being Decadron (the name of her medicine) and the evil villain being cancer. I remember thinking that life after brain surgery wasn't so bad.

Lauren was comforted by the child life specialist's explanation of surgery with this doll.

After surgery, she was covered in love with a feather boa and stuffed animals galore.

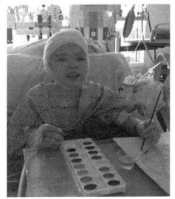

Even after having a brain tumor removed, Lauren was ready for arts and crafts.

CHAPTER 4

"For God so loved the world that he gave his one and only Son, that whoever believes in him shall not perish but have eternal life" John 3:16 NIV.

As much as I felt comforted and loved during our time in the ER and hospital, there was one element that felt out of place. My mom, who has always been my rock and my support, could not be there with us. When Lauren was born, I was living with my mom and dad and I was halfway through nursing school. Because I also had 17-month-old Audrey to look after, my time was stretched thin. From the time Lauren came home from the hospital, my mom became a second mother to Lauren. She fed her, bathed her, and rocked her to sleep. Honestly, she was probably more of a mother to Lauren than I was for the first several months of her life. To say the least, their bond is tight.

Then, 10 years later, when Lauren was diagnosed with cancer and undergoing surgery, the fact that my mom couldn't be there was strange and stressful for both of us. At the time, it felt so wrong that she wasn't there. I was trying to hold it together on my own, but now I can see that God's hand was truly guiding every minute of events.

On the same day that we took Lauren to the hospital, my mom was scheduled to have knee replacement surgery. She had gone in for her routine surgery that morning. Since we all live in different states, my parents in Tennessee and my brother in Florida, my dad had been group texting my brother and I throughout the morning with updates. "Mom's being prepped for surgery," and "She's had sedation,"... that sort of thing. Mid-morning he sent us a text telling us that mom had a reaction to her antibiotic and had trouble breathing. He told us that it was pretty serious for a short time, but that they had managed to get her breathing under control and she was resting. The surgery was temporarily postponed, and the doctor was going to let the sedation wear off before letting mom decide if she wanted to go forward with surgery or reschedule for another day. During that waiting period is when I took Lauren to the hospital and found out about her tumor. I remember thinking that I needed my mom more than anyone else in that moment, as a mom and as a nurse I needed everything she had to offer, but she wasn't available. While I knew immediately that there was a very specific reason that God allowed us to learn of Lauren's tumor on the day my mom was unavailable and unable to even know, I still wanted my mom there.

I was still reeling from the shock of Lauren's diagnosis, and I had not yet gotten to the point of notifying people about her situation, when I received a text from my dad saying that mom had woken up and wanted to go ahead with the surgery, so she was being prepped. I will never forget, staring at that text and realizing that no one knew what was happening on my end of the world.

When I responded to my dad, I didn't even say anything about my mom. All I said was, "I took Lauren to the emergency room and she has a brain tumor." Looking back, I can't believe I was so blunt in my way of telling him that his precious grandbaby was so sick, but in that moment those were the only words that would form.

My dad told me later on that my mom's surgeon had been standing with him when he got my text message, and my dad had fallen to his knees. The surgeon, thinking my dad was worried about my mom, knelt beside him and reassured him that she was going to be okay. When my dad showed him the text I had sent, the surgeon put his arm around my dad and prayed with him.

God knew, and I did too, that the minute my mom found out about Lauren she would hit the road to Atlanta and be right by our side for the long haul. But God also knew something I didn't. God knew that I would need her much more down the road than I did in those first moments, and He knew that they only way to make that happen was to sedate her on the day we found out and keep her physically unable to travel for weeks.

Because we were all so uncertain of what was going on at first, we decided not to tell Audrey and Haley about the possibility of cancer. They knew that there was something in her head that had to come out, and they came to see her at the hospital. They were both 11 at the time, but we quickly realized that with social media word was traveling so fast that it would only take one Facebook post, one text, one comment from a well-meaning visitor, and they would find out from someone else that their little sister had cancer. So we decided to tell them ourselves.

We had the child life specialist from the hospital come in and explain to them what cancer was. Child life specialists are amazing people whose job includes supporting the patient and siblings through play and fun, educating them on an age-appropriate level about what is happening, and helping them express their feelings. I was so worried about how they would take the news, but they were strong and understanding. They asked some questions, and then just said "okay." They didn't seem too worried. It wasn't until the reality of what cancer would do to our family began to hit us that they really understood what was happening.

Telling Lauren though, was much different. When Lauren's cancer journey began, one of the most difficult things to do was to sit down with her and help her to really understand what was happening. My conversation with her went something like this:

> *Lauren, there is an evil thing inside of you, an illness, called cancer. If we do nothing and ignore it, it will grow, and it will harm you. You might even die. The good news is, there is hope. There is a treatment, a fix, a cure. But it won't be easy. The fix itself is harmful to you. Your hair will fall out, you may lose your hearing or go blind. You will most likely have some problems the rest of your life. But you WILL have life! And once the treatment is finished, when the job is done, you will be saved from this evil. And along the way, others will benefit from your experience, and children after you will be saved, too.*

This was such a hard conversation to have, one that no parent ever wants to even think about. I found myself praying fervently, "God, I know somehow You'll get us through, but how? God, help me have strength. I know You can and I know You will, but Lord, help me."

Chapter 4

And alone, in the dark of night, laying in the hospital bed watching my sweet girl sleep, I heard the Lord speak to me. Although it wasn't an audible voice, the message was clear. I could not deny it, for He spoke right to my heart. He said, *Child, I am a parent too. I know where you are. I've been in that same place. I've had that same conversation with my own Son. I know exactly what you're going through and how you feel.*

I wonder if God had a similar conversation with Jesus. I imagine they met one day when Jesus had gone alone to pray, and maybe the conversation went something like this:

Son, there is a sickness in this world, an evil, an illness called sin. If we ignore it and do nothing, it will destroy everyone. But do not fear! There is hope. There is a fix, a treatment, a cure. But this fix, it will hurt you. It will scar your hands and feet, it will batter your body and you will die. But when it is finished, the people will be saved. You will rise again and have life, and many of the people who see you will be saved. Many will be changed because of your experience and your endurance of this fight for the cure. So, Son, because of this, I am choosing to allow you to endure that hardship of treatment, because the end result is a greater good—salvation.

Isn't it wonderful to rest in the comfort of knowing that God understands us? He knows our pain and joy, He understands where we are and what we are going through. When no one else on earth seems to get it, we can crawl into His arms and rest, knowing that He who formed us in our mother's womb, who knows the number of hairs on our head, completely understands us. What an encouragement! I knew that God understood my struggle and would carry me through the most intense emotional ups and downs of my life over the next few months.

CHAPTER 5

"Who stilled the roaring of the seas, the roaring of their waves, and the turmoil of the nations" Psalm 65:7 NIV.

Lauren was discharged from the hospital on a Friday, and our follow-up appointment with the oncologist was scheduled for the following Tuesday. I don't remember the waiting period being particularly difficult. We kept busy over the weekend, and to be honest I think we were still in denial or shock. Things had gone so well thus far.

Brian and I took Lauren to the appointment, where we met with Lauren's dad and her dad's mom. We took the elevator to the fourth floor, and when the doors opened, the wall in front of us held a large sign for the "Aflac Cancer & Blood Disorders Center." Seeing that sign stung a little. The reality was beginning to set in. We exited the elevator into the waiting room and signed in. I scanned the room with my nurse's eyes, and immediately became nauseous.

I saw children bald from chemotherapy, significantly overweight from steroids, pale from illness. I saw parents who were tired, weary, worn. I didn't understand all of the details yet, but I knew I didn't like what I was seeing. Lauren's name was called and we were taken back to get her height and weight measured, and then taken to a private exam room. After a short wait, several people entered the room. There was an oncologist, a social worker, and a child life specialist. The child life specialist took Lauren to a play room so that the adults could talk. I took out a notebook and pen, prepared to take some notes and get the show on the road. I was ready, I was strong, I was certain I could handle this.

The doctor began to speak in a low tone. I could feel the room rocking, like waves raging at sea. I jotted furiously, not wanting to miss a thing. I couldn't write every word, but caught snippets on my page.

AT/RT . . . most aggressive . . . stage four . . . need to check for spread . . . MRI, CT of chest, abdomen, pelvis, kidney, spinal tap, bone marrow test . . . must complete all within three weeks. I flipped to the second page. That was just the intro, now on to the treatment. *Intense . . . 7 on a scale of 1 to 10 . . . about one year if all goes as planned . . . chemo and radiation . . . hair loss, weight loss, tiredness, a lot of hospital time.* Flip to page three. God help us, the doctor's still talking. *Radiation . . . proton . . . not in GA, maybe TX or FL . . . depends on insurance . . . right frontal lobe may affect memory and personality . . . needs chemo through IV and spinal and port on brain . . . needs feeding tube . . . chemo and radiation will lose appetite . . . nutrition concerns.* Page four, and my hand was beginning to cramp. *Staging . . . need CT, heart ultrasound, hearing test, ommaya, GT, port, spinal tap, bone marrow, chemo, neuropsych . . . possible side effects: hearing loss/hearing aids, hormone deficiencies, short stature, learning difficulties.* Page 5. *Need CSF flow study for ommaya surgery, already scheduled . . . physical and occupational therapy.*

Chapter 5

Five pages of frantic notes, five pages telling me that my daughter didn't just have cancer, but an extremely rare and aggressive kind—a cancer that could change everything about her, if she even survived at all. My hand hurt from writing, my head hurt from processing, and my heart hurt from Satan's attack. My ears were burning from all the noise they had just taken in.

We asked a lot questions, I don't remember any of them. The doctor handed us a 15-page packet to review and sign. The packet was titled "Consent for Treatment." Sounds so simple, doesn't it? The packet outlined the 10 different chemotherapy drugs that Lauren would require, each page listing a drug, and then three columns of side effects: Likely, Less Likely, and Rare But Serious. The words began to blur in front of my eyes. I turned back to the first page, mid-section, and began to read.

"What are the alternatives to this treatment? You may choose no therapy at this time. However, if you choose not to receive specific therapy for the disease, the cancer is extremely likely to progress and cause death." I was trying not to vomit at this point. The endless ocean that lay ahead of us was getting bigger by the second. The child life specialist brought Lauren back into the room and explained all of the necessary procedures to her using a doll which had the medical devices inserted that Lauren would be getting. This was actually an effective way to explain the process to her because Lauren loved dolls. It helped her visualize what was going to happen and gave her a chance to ask questions. She laughed, smiled, took it all in stride. We gathered our papers and headed home.

The following three weeks were a whirlwind of appointments amid the process of adjusting to a new pace of life. In those few weeks Lauren had 3 surgeries and 16 doctors' appointments and tests, all just to prepare her body for cancer treatment. I had to set up a Google calendar just to keep up. I began to organize all of the paperwork into three-ring binders.

Just as her doctor had explained, she had a feeding tube inserted because the treatment she would undergo was expected to be so physically intense that she might not be able to feed herself afterward. She also had a port placed in her chest, which is like a permanent version of an IV, so that she wouldn't need an IV inserted for every hospital stay. Then she had another port placed in her brain to deliver chemotherapy directly to the tumor site.

I remember one day, when we were at the hospital for multiple appointments, we had a break in between. We went to the outside play area, and Lauren played basketball for about 30 minutes. The sun was bright and warm, and she was so cheerful. I remember thinking, "How is this really happening to us? She seems so perfectly healthy and happy. This can't be real." A dear friend sent me a text message one night, just when I needed it most. She said, "God is in each detail your heart is in. He is in the trenches with you." In the midst of feeling so inundated with appointments, details and paperwork, it was great to be reminded that God was there with us.

We began to research and learn everything we could about Lauren's cancer. Atypical Teratoid Rhabdoid Tumor, or AT/RT for short, is a rare and very aggressive form of cancer. So rare in fact, that there are only about 100 new cases diagnosed each year. Typically, the symptoms are headache, nausea, and frequent falls—common things that children complain of or demonstrate that most of us brush off as minor. AT/RT is most often seen in children less than three years old, with a survival rate of only 10 – 15%. As age at diagnosis increases, so does the survival rate. The fact that Lauren was nine was a good thing in terms of her chances of survival. Most of the time, AT/RT grows in the brain, but can also be found in the spinal column and kidneys. Thankfully for us, Lauren's cancer was only in one spot, and was nowhere near the brain stem, the control center of the brain. About 50% of kids with AT/RT survive to the five-year post-diagnosis mark, but the intensity of treatment leaves many with lifelong health problems as a result.

Treatment for AT/RT typically involves a combination of surgery, chemotherapy, and radiation. First, surgery is performed if possible to remove the tumor. Fortunately for Lauren, the surgeon was able to remove the entire tumor from her brain. Lauren would undergo 51 weeks on a chemotherapy protocol. The schedule was a bit complicated, but I'll try to explain clearly.

For the first 12 weeks, she had to get a chemotherapy treatment every week. The type of chemo (remember there are 10 different drugs) rotated. Some weeks included between three to five different drugs in combination. Every third week was a five-day chemo regimen, and during the two weeks between them, there was a one-day treatment. For instance, week one included five days in a row of chemotherapy infusions, which meant staying in the hospital for those five days. Weeks two and three had only one day of chemo, so we would spend the day in the outpatient clinic. Then week four was another five-day hospital stay, and so on. Weeks 1 through 6 of this were done in Atlanta, but weeks 7 through 12 also included radiation on Monday through Friday of each week. Since radiation couldn't be done in Atlanta, we would have to go to Jacksonville, Florida for those six weeks. Weeks 13 through 51, back in Atlanta, only required chemo once every three weeks, and the variety of days and number of drugs continued to change over the course of the protocol.

Lauren's type of cancer is ugly and the treatment is barbaric, but the truth is all pediatric cancers are that way. Approximately 2,500 kids in the US die from cancer every year, but the National Cancer Institute spends only about 4% of its budget on childhood cancer research. Many of the treatment protocols being used are the same ones that were used in the 1970s. Pediatric cancer research is significantly underfunded. I encourage you—beg you—to do some research of your own and help in any way you can. At the back of this book are some websites that will give you information about childhood cancer facts and how to help. The bottom line is that childhood cancer is on the rise, more children are being diagnosed than ever before, and we need more help to give our kids the best medical treatments possible.

CHAPTER 6

"Mightier than the thunder of the great waters, mightier than the breakers of the sea—the Lord on high is mighty"
Psalm 93:4 NIV.

Even in the midst of our struggle to come to terms with the cancer that Lauren was facing, we were suddenly surrounded by people who wanted to reach out and help us, dear friends as well as people who we had never met before. Lauren became an instant celebrity in our area. Cards and gifts flooded our home. She had not one, but two gigantic birthday parties, and Lauren had several incredible experiences that she will remember for the rest of her life.

One of the most amazing events took place after we'd gone in for another pre-chemotherapy MRI. Brian's best friend made some calls to people he knew and had arranged for a surprise to be waiting for us when we left the appointment. Audrey and Haley were with us (because they were in on the surprise), and when Lauren woke up from her MRI, there was an Atlanta Hawks fan-mobile waiting for her outside the hospital. A television crew followed us, capturing Lauren's ecstatic reactions, as we made our way to the fan-mobile and were driven to Philips Arena where the Hawks play. Brian, his dad, his step-mom, his best friend (who had arranged this surprise), and his best friend's wife were all waiting for us at the arena.

A lady who works with the Hawks led Lauren into her very own locker room, which was all decked out just for her. They had set up a dinner buffet, with her favorite soft tacos and a huge cookie cake decorated with a big Atlanta hawk on it. She had her own jersey, warm-up suit, bag, and hats for her and her sisters—every kind of Atlanta Hawks gear you can imagine. Lauren was so excited because that night she got to be their "sixth man," so Jeff Teague, the number one player for the Hawks at the time, actually came into her little locker room, talked to her for a bit, and walked her out onto the court with the team. She got to warm up with them, and when they announced the team players at the beginning of the game, they called Lauren's name as a player. They even announced her height and where she was from, just like every other player on the team.

"Introducing Lauren Morris, four feet tall, from Cumming, Georgia!" The Hawks mascot picked her up and showed her to the crowd. She met Dominique Wilkins, which was a dream come true for Brian, and the cheerleaders spent time with her. It was just absolutely amazing to show her that the whole city was behind her. It felt like everybody was on her team and that she was a star. Because we were so new in this journey, we had no idea that opportunities like this would continue to come our way.

When we spent the day with the Hawks we were truly able to bask in the enjoyment and fun of it. We had courtside seats for the game, Jeff Teague was awesome with Lauren—on and off the court—and they made Lauren feel so special.

Chapter 6

In that moment, we felt that we could still easily have joy in the midst of all this, because that was before the hit came, before we had recognized our new reality. All we knew is that we'd left an MRI, been escorted to a Hawks' game, and the next morning we were back to the regiment of multiple appointments that were preparing Lauren's body for the upcoming chemotherapy.

That transition time, with so many appointments, scattered with gifts and surprises, was almost a surreal high. We had no clue how low the valley was that we were about to go through. The adrenaline kept us going, and the sudden attention from so many people brought a sense of security and goodness. We were still outsiders to the pediatric cancer world, so naive about what was coming. There is a reason that God doesn't give us too much information at once. One day at a time is often all we can handle.

After the month of prep work, April came, and it was time to begin Lauren's treatment protocol. It would take one to one-and-a-half years to complete, depending on her tolerance and potential setbacks. When the doctor explained the schedule to us, I could barely grasp what 51 weeks of treatment would look and feel like. Until you've lived through it, there is no possible way to understand or explain it.

Anchors for Hope

Lauren was a celebrity!

CHAPTER 7

"God is our refuge and strength, an ever-present help in trouble" Psalm 46:1 NIV.

April 9, 2014, was the first day of treatment, and overall it was a good day. We arrived early in the morning at the Aflac Cancer Clinic. The first step was to access Lauren's port. In simple terms, this means that a large needle has to be placed through Lauren's chest and into the implanted device. Lauren's port access went well, but the port itself was not cooperating.

The nurse gave her some medicine in an effort to improve the function, and while we waited for it to take effect, she had to start an IV. Lauren handled this extremely well. After she was sedated for spinal tap and spinal chemo, I sent a quick text to my dad, asking for him to pray for the port to work. If it didn't work, this could mean that the port would have to be surgically removed and a new one put in. 10 minutes later, the nurse came out and told us that the spinal chemo was done, Lauren did great, and that the port was working. God had faithfully answered our prayers.

We then moved into the infusion area of the clinic while Lauren continued to sleep off her sedation. When she woke up she complained of a tummy ache, so the nurse gave her some nausea medicine. Back to sleep she went, and I said a quick prayer asking God to minimize her chemo side effects. When she woke up again a few hours later, the nausea was completely gone, and she was hungry enough to eat an entire hamburger. I was so encouraged that her body seemed to be responding well to the first dose of chemotherapy.

The chemo given through her chest port that day lasted a total of about six hours. Initially, Lauren had no side effects. She played on her iPad, did word searches, and watched movies. The next three days consisted of about one hour's worth of IV chemo each morning, and then playing and hanging out in the afternoons.

Days 2, 3, and 4 of the first week brought nausea, leg pain, and sores in her mouth and throat. Days 3 and 4 of chemo were the hardest days of my entire life up to that point, and of Lauren's too. Watching my child scream in pain and beg me to make it stop was agonizing, even worse was the fact that I had signed consent for this. I allowed this treatment to take place. I chose to put her through this misery. Yet there was absolutely nothing I could do to comfort her. She didn't even want me to hold her and comfort her. I could barely touch her without her raw nerves feeling intense pain.

I called my dad on April 12, one month since diagnosis, at 12:30 AM, and woke him up with my sobs, telling him that I just didn't know if I could bear this pain. I asked him to pray for my strength, and he promised he would. My dad is the most amazing, tenderhearted man. As a firefighter and an extremely generous man, he is a hero to many people, and he was my hero throughout our cancer journey.

Chapter 7

When Lauren was finally sleeping peacefully, I was able to lie down for once in the dark, quiet room and just be still. Isn't that what God asks us to do? "Be still and know that I am God." Yes He is, and He reminded me in that still quiet moment that He knew exactly how I felt. He chose to send His only Son to the cross to suffer so that others might be healed. He chose not to intervene or stop it, even when Jesus asked. And Mary, dear, sweet Mary, she knew the pain of my mother's heart. She felt the agony as she watched her son being crucified. I knew in that moment that I was not alone.

I remembered thinking back to that old *Footprints* poem by Mary Stevenson. I had always thought it was just a sort of cheesy poem about Jesus, but in that quiet room, I began to understand. I had not walked one footstep of this journey, my God had carried me.

In the weeks leading up to chemotherapy, I spent much of my time in deep thought, a whirlwind of emotions and observations swirling through my head. With every step of testing and potential side effects, the Great Physician displayed His works, and my faith was strengthened. When I felt overwhelmed and scared, Abba Father comforted me. When I was exhausted and trying to stay awake to drive to yet another early morning appointment, the Prince of Peace guided sweet Lauren to start singing from the back seat, "My God is so big and so strong and so mighty, there's nothing my God cannot do!"

Please don't misunderstand me, my faith was not naive. I did not see through rose-colored glasses. I was very much aware that we were walking through the valley of the shadow of death. My experiences as a PICU nurse sometimes haunted me as I walked

Anchors for Hope

this journey with my own child. There were tough days. Every time I looked at my phone, I got so angry at Apple for making a "Favorites" list in Contacts. It should be called something else, like "Important Contacts" because Aflac Cancer Center should be *no one's* favorite! I hated watching my baby girl bravely push her own IV pole around a hospital room. I hated being in the unit that tugs so hard at peoples' hearts that they form organizations simply around providing catered meals to patients' families on a regular basis. I could hardly believe we were in a unit in the hospital that was designed for extended stays, with extra-large rooms, a desk at which parents could work or a child could do homework, bathrooms with shelves for all your toiletries.

As I absorbed all of this, sometimes, in my mind, I would shout, "THIS IS NOT FAIR! THIS STINKS!" The cancer journey is painful, scary, and full of burden. It weighs heavy on your soul and adds years to your life. And yet you learn to appreciate every second of life, every precious moment, every sassy, smart-mouth comment that your little princess makes. You begin to treasure every moment with your other children, because you never know when something will steal your time from them.

Still, through all of this, a quiet voice whispered, "I am here." God was faithful to us. He provided comfort for my pain, reassurance for my fear, and relief from my burden. He gave us an abundance of family, friends, and caring nurses and doctors who lifted us up daily with encouragement and prayers. And most importantly, God provided hope. I didn't know until those dark nights at the hospital how much my soul needed hope. I remember how I used to correct the girls when they prayed. If they said, "Dear Lord, we hope that . . ." I would tell them to ask God to please *help*, and not to just *hope* that something will happen. But I should have known that childlike faith was right all along. So many times in the Bible we are told to HOPE in the Lord, and I was learning to cling to that HOPE with all my heart.

Week two of chemotherapy was much better than week one. Lauren was sick immediately following treatment and had a rough afternoon, but she was feeling much better by bedtime. We had also started giving IV fluids at home, and that helped as well. Someone posted a Bible verse on Facebook that day that really caught my attention.

Psalm 46:1 says, "God is our refuge and strength, a very present help in trouble." I had always focused on the refuge, strength, and help in this verse. However, when I read it that time, it was as if God was highlighting the word "present" for me. He isn't some far off God sending down feel-good wishes. He isn't a statue, idol, or dead prophet who I pray to and trust in. He is a Living God. Present. He is right here with us, among us, in the midst of our lives. What a great comfort that is!

With the introduction of cancer, our home changed dramatically. Our living room became a recovery room. Lauren had a cozy setup on the couch, and medicines and supplies filled our coffee table. At the time, Lauren and Haley had a shared room and Audrey had her own room. The two rooms were joined by a Jack-and-Jill bathroom. When Lauren was diagnosed we immediately began making plans to put Audrey and Haley together in the larger room and Lauren by herself. We knew we would need a space for Lauren's care and a separate room to keep her way from germs. This was also the room closest to ours.

Lauren's elementary school staff surprised us and donated funds for a room makeover. Her art teacher even came out to paint murals on the bedroom walls to make the rooms into a beautiful, fun retreat for all three girls.

Once the rooms were finished, we moved all of Lauren's medicines and supplies from the coffee table into her own room. The lavender butterfly retreat became a makeshift hospital room. An IV pole next to her bed held fluids and a feeding pump. A mini fridge was placed under her desk to hold refrigerated medications. Her under-sink space held gauze, syringes, bottles, medical tape, a special mouthwash, and countless skin creams. We placed a large plastic basket on the bathroom counter to hold medications. We tried to choose a pretty one, so it wouldn't feel so much like a hospital bin, but the size alone reminded us constantly of just how sick she was. The medicine box was 12 inches wide, 16 inches long, and 8 inches high, and it was full.

Over time Lauren's closet became stuffed with supplies. We didn't know it yet, but after months of chemotherapy treatment we would need to fill her closet with every kind of shoe and boot imaginable for her many broken feet, braces for her weak wrists, and casts for her various brittle bones. We also stored an entire box of supplies just for Lauren's home nurse. Supplies began to fill our garage as well. Over the coming months, we would line a walker, a wheelchair, a knee scooter, and a stroller along the wall.

The supply stock eventually became so massive that her room couldn't contain them. My neighbor and her small group from church came to our home to help. They bought storage totes, drawers, and supplies. They organized an entire closet with all of Lauren's supplies separated, labeled, and carefully stored in Rubbermaid drawer organizers and totes.

Chapter 7

The blessing of that work was immense.

When Lauren got sick, we were in the middle of renovating our master bedroom closet. Of course that became completely unimportant, so we stopped with a bare room with no shelves or rods for holding our clothes. The same small group from my neighbor's church donated a clothing system from Home Depot and installed it for us. It's true that this was a complete luxury. We did not need a closet system to survive. We would have been fine without a closet at all. For goodness' sake, people live in far worse conditions, but our bare room and disorganized piles of clothes served as a daily visual reminder of cancer stopping us in our tracks. That room stared at us, like cancer's way of laughing in our faces. For this kind group of people to recognize that and step into fix it was huge. Christ provided a victory over Satan in that very practical demonstration for us.

CHAPTER 8

"For our struggle is not against flesh and blood, but against the rulers, against the authorities, against the powers of this dark world and against the spiritual forces of evil in the heavenly realms." Ephesians 6:12 NIV

Halfway through the second week of treatment, the harsh reality really began to set in. By this point in Lauren's cancer journey, she began having tremendous bone pain and was beginning to lose her hair. Every morning there would be another handful left on her pillow. Audrey and Haley cut their long hair down to shoulder length to show their support. She didn't like losing her hair, but it was so minor compared to the other side effects she was enduring that she didn't give it much attention. It wasn't until after treatment was finished and her hair started growing back that she really started to focus on it.

At this point, she was just emotionally and physically drained. Lauren had to be taken to the hospital one night because she had developed a 103-degree fever. In the childhood cancer world, any fever over 101 is considered an emergency, so much so that the emergency room will immediately move an oncology patient ahead of other waiting patients and into a private room due to the high risk. The doctor immediately started her on antibiotics and kept her overnight.

The next day, her grandparents and sisters came to visit. She was not feeling well, and was in a lot of pain. I'll never forget it. I helped her to the bathroom, which was a feat in itself because she was so weak and in so much pain. While sitting on the toilet, I practically had to hold her up. Then she started having trouble breathing. I looked at the student nurse, who was standing in our doorway, and said, "We need to get her on the monitor, call her nurse." I picked her up and carried her back to her bed, and began hooking her up to the monitor to check her heart rate and breathing.

As I was hooking her up to the monitor she went limp and stopped breathing. The nurse and student nurse were just walking in and began to take over. My brain went into full nurse mode. I looked at my mother-in-law, pointed to Audrey and Haley, and said, "Take them home." I glanced back for just a second to see Brian frozen in the corner of the room, paralyzed by the sudden change. He had learned medical terminology and skills beyond his imagination in the last few months, but this was something he had never seen before. I locked eyes with him for a second, as if to tell him that I would handle this, and then my attention was back to Lauren. The nurses had been able to stimulate her to start breathing again and were watching her closely. She continued to go in and out of consciousness while having short periods of apnea (not breathing). Her nurse decided to call the hospital's rapid response team to get another set of eyes on her and a second opinion.

The rapid response team is comprised of an ICU nurse and respiratory therapist. They came to Lauren's room and did an assessment and some quick blood tests. During this time she continued to have periods of confusion, memory loss, and extreme anxiety. She started to scream and cry, then she blacked out and stopped breathing. When the nurse or doctor tried to stimulate her to breathe, she would sit straight up and scream, "Why are you hurting me?!" We tried to comfort her, but nothing was working. Her body eventually calmed, although she was still not alert.

After a few hours of this madness, with doctors and nurses in and out constantly, she began to smile, and tears ran down her cheeks. I was on one side of the bed talking to her, and the chaplain was on the other. Lauren said, "I see a glowing man, he wants me to come to him. He wants me to come up the glass stairs, and Nana Nana is there with him, and another lady too, and a puppy! The red man wants me too, but he looks scary." She wasn't aware of where she was or who she was talking to. It was as if her mind was in another realm completely, and we were bearing witness.

I was terrified of what was about to happen. I told her, reluctantly, to go to the glowing man if he called to her, all the while begging God in my mind not to take my baby from me. I knew that "red man" all too well. His evil schemes were the source of this whole mess. Satan couldn't hide from me, and I would not let him take my baby. I will fight to the death for my kids and my marriage.

This whole event went on for almost four hours. After trying several medications and interventions without resolve, Lauren was taken to get a CT scan to make sure there wasn't anything new in her brain, then on to the PICU. The CT scan was good, and the EEG they did overnight to look for seizure activity was also fine. She got a platelet transfusion and a blood transfusion, both of which had been expected with the chemo treatment.

The next day Lauren's breathing was back to normal and she had no more of this seizure-like activity. I asked her if she remembered anything that had happened the night before, and she said she only remembered dreaming about Jesus asking her to come up the glass stairs, handing her a cloud, and then telling her to go back to her mommy. I had chills. God had revealed Himself directly to her. It was as if He had allowed her some out of body experience, where she was able to glimpse heaven and receive peace that was impossible to obtain here on earth. For the first time in my life, I understood just how real and present spiritual warfare was.

When Lauren was experiencing that episode (for lack of a better word), she had seemed so scared. She would scream at me to make it stop, make it better. I tried to calm her and explain to her what we were doing to help her, like running tests or moving rooms, but she did not want to hear the process. She only wanted me to fix it right then and there, and when I told her that I couldn't, she got so angry at me.

Isn't that exactly how we treat God? We find ourselves in a desperate situation and cry out for a quick fix. We don't want to know His plan, His process, we just want Him to do what we ask of Him, and we want Him to do it now. Many times we don't get that, and instead of resting in the comfort and trust of His plan, we get angry with Him. If only we could learn to let go and just trust Him when He assures us that it will be okay, that He is there with us, and that our struggle will subside.

When Lauren was being prepped for the CT scan, she told me she was so scared, and so I told her I would stand at her feet and pray over her so she could hear my voice. I had no idea what else I could do at the moment, and prayer had become another coping strategy that I relied on heavily. Most often, my prayers were simple requests, "make her stop throwing up," "let her stop itching tonight." I was desperate too. She asked if she could pray too, and of course I said yes.

She cried out in a loud voice, "God heal me, heal me so I can praise you!" I was so surprised, but I fully believe that the Holy Spirit living in her was doing a mighty work in her heart and mind through this process. And I'm so glad He did.

After Lauren's visions, she asked me to paint a picture of what she described to me. She saw her deceased grandmother and great grandmother, and a glowing man. I told her, with tears lodged in my throat, to go to the glowing man, if He called to her.

Lauren grew spiritually throughout her cancer journey. She would ask to go pray during the day. I'd wheel her into the chapel, and if she had the strength, she'd get down on her knees to pray for all of the sick children in the hospital and for anyone who didn't know Jesus to find Him. My little girl showed me what true, enduring faith looks like.

CHAPTER 9

"Even though I walk through the valley of the shadow of death, I fear no evil, for You are with me" Psalm 23:4. NASB

On May 7, 2014, Lauren started her fourth chemo treatment, and it was particularly tough round. Nausea and vomiting from the previous week's treatment caused Lauren to lose weight. This was very concerning, because her body could barely tolerate the chemotherapy doses from the beginning, and losing weight would reduce her body's ability to function during treatment, or even her ability to survive. If the chemotherapy doses had to be reduced, her chances of survival would also be reduced. Her doctors were worried enough that they planned to put in a different type of feeding tube, one that would bypass her stomach and go straight into her intestines, in hopes of allowing her body to better maintain weight. We already had plans to travel straight to Jacksonville, Florida after chemotherapy that day for appointments with her radiation oncologist in preparation for her upcoming radiation, so her oncologist planned to change the feeding tube after we got back.

After the treatment was finished, my mom, Lauren, and I immediately hit the road to Jacksonville. God had so perfectly timed my mom's recovery from knee surgery that she was well enough to be able to travel with us to Jacksonville. We settled into a hotel, hoping for a good night's sleep.

The next morning, we met the general oncologist who would care for her in Jacksonville and the radiation oncologist who would be overseeing Lauren's radiation treatments, and Lauren was fitted for her radiation mask. We also checked out our housing options while we were there, praying that God would make clear to us where we needed to stay during our six-week treatment, which was supposed to begin May 21. Our plan for this three-day trip was to complete the last oncology appointment, finalize a place to rent for the upcoming six weeks of radiation, and head home to pack for our return in two weeks.

The appointments went well. The area in Lauren's brain where the tumor was located had healed so well, that the radiation oncologist wanted to capitalize on this and start treatment early. In order to make that happen, Lauren had to have an MRI that night. It was very late, and the hospital staff was difficult to work with. We had to wait in the waiting area for over an hour, and Lauren was so sick that I was getting frustrated. Why would they make her wait so long when our appointment was already late? The staff was unapologetic and didn't seem to understand her or the situation. Being that the children's hospital is only a section of the main hospital, I already had concerns about not having an all-pediatric staff. Anxiety was building up in me and piling onto the fear I already had for Lauren's treatment.

Chapter 9

When it was finally time for her to be sedated, the tech came out and said she needed to start an IV. We explained to her that Lauren had a port and therefore did not need an IV, but needed her port accessed instead. The tech proceeded to tell me that they did not have anyone working that late who could access a port.

I was floored. We were in a *hospital*, and she was telling me there wasn't a nurse anywhere in the building? I almost lost it, but thankfully my mom was there to keep me somewhat calm. With Lauren watching my every move, I was cautious not to show too much concern or frustration for fear of upsetting her. I asked to speak to the house supervisor, and they said they would call. An hour later I had heard from no one and we were still waiting. So I asked again. This time, I stood by the tech until she picked up the phone and called.

When the house supervisor came down, she was very upset at how things had been handled thus far, and she called the pediatric cancer unit to have a nurse come down and access Lauren's port. She assured us that this was not normal for their hospital and that we would have a much better experience going forward. I prayed that she was telling the truth, but my gut told me otherwise. That instinct was something I had learned to listen to carefully and to take very seriously.

Finally, a nurse came down to access her port, and the MRI itself was uneventful. Friday, after the last oncology appointment, we were able to secure our apartment for the long stay, and my mom and I were ready to head back to Atlanta. But Lauren begged us to go see the beach before driving home, so we decided to stay in the area one more night.

Anchors for Hope

Jacksonville Beach, about 30 minutes away, was hosting a large golf tournament, so hotel options were extremely limited, but we found one of the last rooms and set out for an evening at the beach.

I'm so glad we put forth the extra effort to get to Jacksonville Beach because for a full 45 minutes at the hotel that evening, Lauren was her old self, laughing, singing, and designing her wedding dress. The three of us snuggled up in the king size bed and watched Say Yes to the Dress on TV. Lauren described to my mom and me every detail of what she wanted her wedding dress to look like, and giggled at some of the crazy requests of the brides on TV. We all got to bed early, with plans to walk the beach early Saturday morning before heading back to Atlanta.

The thing about childhood cancer is that it laughs in the face of your so-called plans. At 2:30 AM a splash of hot vomit on my chest awoke me. Lauren was sick with a 103 degree fever—automatic emergency.

My mom put Lauren in a cool bath while I cleaned myself up. I then drove Lauren the 30 minutes back to the Jacksonville emergency room, leaving mom behind to handle the mess. Lauren was admitted to the cancer unit, and her temperature remained between 101 and 104. She also had to get blood and platelet transfusions due to her counts being low. The next morning, after Lauren was settled and stable, I drove back to the hotel to get my mom.

The trip took me about an hour, and I have never felt as awful as I did in that moment, leaving Lauren alone in an unfamiliar hospital for that hour. I knew she was in good hands with a great nurse, but she's my baby. Having my mom abandoned in a hotel and my baby sick in a hospital in a city I knew nothing about

Chapter 9

was the worst feeling I've ever experienced. I hated Jacksonville already, and I couldn't stomach the reality of having to come back in just two weeks for a six-week stay in this place. It was all I could do to get through the drive.

When my mom and I arrived back at the hospital, my nightmare got even worse. The doctor told us that Lauren would have to be hospitalized for at least three days. The feeding tube surgery would have to be scheduled for Jacksonville, in a hospital that I already disliked, instead of Atlanta, in a hospital that I trusted. To make the situation even more stressful, her radiation oncologist wanted to start radiation early, which meant that we would not be going back to Atlanta at all. Our three-day trip just turned into an eight-week visit to hell.

We were stuck in Jacksonville for eight more weeks. I wanted to die. Seriously. My baby was dying in front of my eyes, and my mom and I had no place to stay. We had come to Jacksonville with only three days of clothes and supplies. I had left Audrey, Haley, and Brian behind for what I thought was a long weekend, only to find out that it was really for two months. Audrey and Haley would graduate fifth grade without me, my husband would somehow have to manage work, the girls' activities at two different schools, the puppy, and the house . . . this was all too much. I was at my lowest. The reality of the hell we were living in hit me like a slap in the face on an icy day.

I remember having a conversation about our relationship and the strain that was mounting. I said, "I can't possibly fight for my child's life and fight for my marriage at the same time. We just have to decide that we will make it. We just have to endure."

Lauren was miserable with pain. Her fever was dangerously high, and I was no help. My mom and I were both exhausted from the pace of chemotherapy and appointments we had kept over the last several days, and I could not for the life of me find evidence of God in this hideous town. I was so desperate for something good that we celebrated when her fever was between 101 and 102 because that was better than where we had started. There was no escaping this treacherous road. There was no break, no getaway. Lauren's needs were 24/7, and therefore so was my effort.

Then God showed me. He showed me that he wasn't only there with us at that moment but he had been preparing the way for years in advance. Two of my neighbors reached out, saying that they just happened to be traveling to Jacksonville for business and would be happy to pick up a suitcase from Brian and bring it with them. A dear friend of my mom's contacted one of her best friends, who lived near Jacksonville. She then worked with her church group to provide meals and groceries for us over the next eight weeks. My stepdaughter's mom took my oldest daughter in as one of her own, helping get her to and from school and celebrating her last year of elementary school with her. The apartment complex manager allowed us to move in early so that we could have a home. One of my neighbors baked a cake and another took balloons to our house for Brian's birthday. God provided in ways I could never have imagined.

Chapter 9

Lauren wanted desperately to see the beach, and I'm so glad we made the extra effort to drive through a storm to see the ocean. She was all smiles, and it was the last time she would feel so good for months.

Chapter 10

"There is a time for everything, and a season for every activity under the heavens" Ecclesiastes 3:1 NIV.

There is absolutely no way that Lauren or I would have made it through our stint in Jacksonville if it weren't for my mom. God's plan for her retirement fit right into our timeline, and I have no doubt that that was on purpose. It was so taxing to endure the physical and emotional ups and downs that each day brought, but my mom did it with a smile. My mom is an angel on earth, an amazing Godly woman, who approaches each day with grace and dignity, hope and love. All who know her are blessed by her. While in Jacksonville, I realized that God had allowed me the unique and precious opportunity of practicing nursing alongside my mom, who was my inspiration as a nurse. Her wisdom is astounding, and she cares for others with such gentleness that truly embodies the spirit of nursing. It was truly an honor to watch her and learn from her in her craft.

And even though we were going through hell, God reminded us that there was still good in the world. It's incredibly difficult to sort through the emotions of childhood cancer. There is an overshadowing gray cloud that taints every part of the world you live in. But God sprinkles joy in amongst the clouds. We learned to celebrate moments of happiness in our lives and the lives of others as we struggled day by day, hour by hour, and sometimes even minute by minute.

Shortly after our arrival in Jacksonville, my brother and his wife received word that they could finally travel to Korea to bring home my adopted niece. They had waited years for her, and the time had finally come. My brother and I had a long conversation about the topic that God had been pressing on my heart for several years. I really felt God teaching me to enjoy the good times. Ecclesiastes 3:1–8 explains that there is truly a time for everything, for "every event under heaven." While I was watching my youngest child fight for her life, and watching the effects of childhood cancer on my family, my precious brother and sister-in-law were planning for trips to Korea to bring home their adopted daughter. While I was mourning and begging God for mercy, they were celebrating and praising God for His goodness. While they were constantly encouraging me to have faith in my struggle, I was encouraging them to cherish this time of happiness. But one thing was the same for both of us—God's presence.

God is good! While I was walking with my daughter through the vast dark ocean, they were experiencing beautiful blessings in their lives. But what was so amazing, so awesome, so inspiring was that Jesus Christ met us both where we were. And because of that, I was able to share in their joy, just as they shared in my sorrow. We were able to experience God's goodness together, in weeping and in laughter, mourning and dancing.

The conversation with my brother sparked a new mindset for me. I began to look more deeply into areas of joy in my own life that I had previously overlooked. Spending Mother's Day in Jacksonville was a time of great reflection for me. Never had I been more honored to claim the title of mother. On that day, I wrote in a journal:

> *My children inspire me, they teach me, and they make me so much better than I ever could have been without them. Audrey makes me laugh, lifts me up, and has taught me to give 100% to EVERY part of life. Haley is so tenderhearted, encouraging, and she has taught me to chill out and enjoy life. Lauren has challenged me, pushed me, pointed out so many of my weaknesses, and then given me beautifully detailed suggestions on how to make myself better. In the last eight weeks, all three of my girls have been incredible, each of them using their own strengths to make this family stronger.*

I still feel the truth of this reflection, even today.

Lauren was able to have her feeding tube surgery, but we had trouble with it the entire weekend. She ended up having to have it changed out several more times over the course of our time in Jacksonville. It was a constant struggle and nuisance for us, another reason for me to hate that place. Lauren wanted to eat so badly, but her body rejected every attempt.

When Lauren finally started radiation treatment, we were actually excited. We knew that we had to endure 30 treatments, and each one completed meant we were one day closer to going home. We even made a paper chain with 30 links to hang in the apartment so that we could remove one after every treatment. The treatments were scheduled for every day, Monday through Friday, for six weeks. She did great with her first radiation day and even came out smiling. The radiation oncologist was very pleased with the radiation dose and location that she was able to create for Lauren's treatment, which meant the side effects should be minimal down the road. For that we were thankful, but thinking about "down the road" was such a non-event for us because we were struggling so hard just to get through the "now."

The next six weeks consisted of daily radiation Monday through Friday, weekly chemotherapy, physical therapy, clinic appointments for lab work, and of course some unplanned hospitalizations. Fortunately or unfortunately—I don't know which—we had started to figure out a pattern by this point, and we were able to predict most of the "unplanned hospitalizations" within a day or two.

One day, Lauren was craving Cracker Barrel chicken and dumplings. Taking advantage of the opportunity for a few minutes of alone time to clear my head, I volunteered to make the drive while my mom stayed with Lauren. While waiting for our food, I noticed a book sitting on a table beside the register. The title was *God Will Carry You Through* by Max Lucado. Quite honestly, I picked it up because it had a pretty cover. I had just enough money on a gift card from a friend, so I bought the book along with the food, and went back to the apartment.

Lauren liked for me to read to her, so when I opened the book and began to read it out loud, I knew that the book was placed in my sight for a reason. The first page of the book said this, "You'll get through this. It won't be painless. It won't be quick. But God will use this mess for good. Don't be foolish or naïve. But don't despair either. With God's help, you will get through this." God was with us, and He was showing me His presence, little by little.

Several doses into radiation, Lauren began having some anxiety when she went into the machine. These proton radiation

Chapter 10

machines are hard to describe, but suffice it to say that my brief tour of the room felt more like a visit to NASA then a medical facility. I mentioned Lauren's anxiety on a blog post when updating our family and friends, and within a few days our apartment mailbox was flooded with Christian music CDs for her to listen to during treatment. What a huge and unexpected help that was. Anything we needed, at any time, was provided to us in one way or another. God had everything covered.

God continued to be the master orchestrator, in control of all things, and He showed His mercy to me in little things, but those little things meant so much to me. Lauren was diagnosed with her brain tumor on March 11, 2014. Due to Lauren's weight loss and overall weakness, we started praying specifically that we would be able to find a stroller for her. That may seem like an odd thing to pray for, but it's surprisingly difficult to find a good stroller for older children. Most cancer patients have to use wheelchairs, but riding in a wheelchair hurt Lauren's back and legs after only a few days, and, honestly, it killed my back when I was lifting it in and out of the car. And just the idea of riding in a wheelchair weighed heavily on her mental toughness, making her feel sick just from knowing she depended on it. On top of that, it wouldn't even fit in my car.

After radiation one day, we went to Babies R Us and immediately found a stroller that Lauren loved. Finding that stroller was exciting for me. When we got back to the apartment, I went online to enter the registration for the warranty, and had to enter the date of manufacture. Brace yourself—the date was March 10, 2014. Yes, *the day before* God revealed this journey to us, He placed the parts for this stroller in the hands of the perfect assembler and orchestrated it to be shipped to this store location, *right where He knew we would be.*

With additional chemotherapy treatments came other additional side effects. Lauren began to experience burn-like wounds on her hands, leaving them raw and painful. Her left eyelid began to droop, and we had some problems with the Jacksonville oncologist not taking care of all of her needs. Fortunately, my mother-in-law was able to come stay with us for a week while my mom went home, and she took wonderful care of us. She cooked for us and comforted us, and helped manage the household in our apartment so I could focus on Lauren. She filled my soul with much needed love and rejuvenation.

Consistency in the midst of chaos became a comfort to us, even the seemingly negative consistency. Fevers came every 10 days after chemotherapy, so we could count on them and plan for them. In fact there was only one chemotherapy treatment throughout the entire 51 weeks that didn't result in a fever hospitalization. We were in and out of the hospital frequently with fevers, and her body continued to wear down from the struggle and harsh treatments. Her kidneys began to weaken, so we had to make additional adjustments to her treatment schedule. As things slowly progressed, I felt her little body slowly slipping further and further into disability. I was watching her die a slow death. Her once healthy body now looked like a skeleton draped in a thin sheet of skin. Her personality was hidden by pain, the hours in her day stolen by weakness and exhaustion.

On a particular day, when we were struggling with her new kidney issues and I was worried sick about what else might go wrong, Lauren asked me to read to her from a new book she had received. Once again God shocked me right on page one, which read, "Have you ever wondered who God is? Our God, who lives in heaven, made the sun and all the wonderful things we see. He makes everything work together to help us live and grow so well." God reminded us that He made our bodies so that our kidneys would work together with our other organs to help us live. Lauren's body already had the miraculous finger print of God's handmade design. He has always been way ahead of us.

One of the toughest things to watch change over time was Lauren's weight. When she was diagnosed with brain cancer in March of 2014, Lauren weighed approximately 45 pounds. Within two months, she had lost 10 pounds and looked like a skeleton. She was too weak to walk and had to be carried and lifted everywhere she went. As the months went on, medications and complications caused her to go up to 60 pounds, back down to 45, and eventually up to 75. The stress this put on her body and joints over time has created pain, breathing trouble, and lots of discomfort.

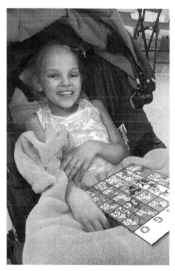

This stroller was, truly, a gift from God.

CHAPTER 11

"May the God of hope fill you with all joy and peace as you trust in him, so that you may overflow with hope by the power of the Holy Spirit" Romans 15:13 NIV.

With each passing day, I also began to notice how Lauren's journey was changing her emotionally and maturing her spirit. The sweet, naïve, innocent baby girl who had been diagnosed with brain cancer was becoming a young lady, wise beyond her years. She could analyze every doctor's tone and facial expression. She could spout off every medication she took and when it was due. She could explain her treatment protocol, risks and side effects, concerns, positives and negatives. She became extremely intuitive and could offer solutions to problems that blew my mind. When someone was down, she would lift them up and encourage them. When I would read to her from her devotion book or Bible, she would close her eyes and smile the most angelic smile. I had known since the day she was born that God had something special in store for her, and I was beginning to see it.

For about a year or so before her diagnosis, I had been wrestling with God over my faith and relationship with Him. My argument went something like this:

> *God, if I strengthen my faith anymore and grow closer to You, I'm afraid that You will allow me to endure something that will test and demonstrate that deep faith and trust. I don't want to do that. I want to be close to You, but I don't want to endure hardship. I have no doubt that I will remain steadfast in my love for You, but I don't want You to make me prove it. If You take someone close to my heart, I will continue to rely on You and know that the separation is only temporary. I am not afraid of that because my hope is eternal. I just don't want to do it and if I trust You deeper, I know You well enough to know that You might use me to show that to others who don't know You.*

God continued to remind me that He had prepared me for such a time as this. Because I had become a pediatric intensive care nurse immediately after graduating from nursing school, the thought of losing a child crossed my mind often. I had walked that road with so many other parents. Yet God used that frequent exposure to prepare my heart and mind for what I would be dealing with when Lauren got sick. God allowed me to wrestle with Him over the issue of deepening my relationship with Him and whether it was worth it. Now I know it was definitely worth it, and I'm grateful He was so patient while I worked to figure that out.

Shortly into Lauren's cancer journey, someone asked me what the "worst case" diagnosis was for Lauren, and I didn't really have an answer. God was in control, and I knew He had her heart, so there really was no "worst case." While she lived, she loved Him, and in death she would live with Him. Lauren taught me that. But even with the reassurance of a final good ending, the day to day struggle remained. And the hardest part is that your status can change in a second. Life with cancer is so unstable.

Chapter 11

I remember a Tuesday evening in Jacksonville, when I was really feeling down. Lauren was sick and Audrey and Haley were on their way home from the beach with my best friend. My friend and her family had completely changed their family vacation to be close to us, but Lauren and I hadn't been able to spend time with them because of Lauren's hospitalization. And to top it all off, Audrey was sick too.

I was having a major pity party. My hope tank was running near empty. I was completely frustrated with the care Lauren was receiving from the Jacksonville oncology group, and I was terrified that any wrong move would be detrimental to her survival. I felt like the weight was all on my shoulders to monitor the moves, but I had no idea what was right or wrong. My nurse- and mom-brains were stretched to their limits. I had reached out to Lauren's Atlanta oncologist out of desperation. I trusted her every word, and I felt like my child's life was in her hands. I needed her intervention. Somehow, that Monday night, I missed her call. I expected a return call Tuesday, and it didn't come, which wasn't like her at all, so I was even more frustrated.

But true to form, God's timing was perfect. I received a call from the doctor Wednesday morning, exactly when I needed it. Had I gotten the same call Tuesday evening, I would have been too tired and weary to appreciate the information she gave. God knew that after a good night's rest my heart and mind would be ready for uplifting news. She said she was very encouraged by Lauren's overall tolerance of her chemotherapy and radiation treatment in Jacksonville. She also said that the electrolyte imbalances and kidney problems were not uncommon for the intensity of her chemotherapy protocol, and that they should eventually resolve themselves. Because we expected all of this to get worse before it got better, our prayer was that she would be able to maintain her full prescribed dosage of chemotherapy to give her the best chance of beating the cancer for good.

During one of her brief breaks from the hospital in Jacksonville, Lauren was well enough to have some fun. It was only a two-day break, but we had a great time shopping and playing at Build-A-Bear. Lauren absolutely loves stuffed animals, so this was a huge comfort to her. The biggest excitement came when we were finally able to fulfill her wish to see the beach. If you remember, the last time we'd spent the night at Jacksonville Beach, Lauren had developed a fever and vomiting during the night, so we never had the chance to have our morning walk on the beach like we'd planned. Since we had one more day for her break, we started driving to Jacksonville Beach with a heavy rain pounding on our windshield. But God dried the sky just in time for my sweet girl to see the beach.

As soon as we came up over the hill and she saw the ocean, her eyes lit up like a morning sunrise. She stopped and stared, then turned around and said, "Take my picture mommy!" I couldn't even see the camera screen through my tears. We had a good 15-minute walk on the beach before she tired out. The weather was perfect and cool enough for her to enjoy. The rain had driven away the crowd, so she was able to truly relax. I felt like getting her to the beach was one of the greatest accomplishments of my life. She enjoyed the beach so much that we went back twice. I was afraid that with all the medications she had to take and her inability to swim or play in the sand due to her tubes and lines she might get depressed, but she sported her swimsuit and cute cover up like a rock star, and laid on her beach towel under an umbrella for two hours straight. She just kept smiling and saying, "This is so relaxing, this is so nice!" She even was able to get her feet in the water and enjoy the waves for a few minutes.

She was learning to appreciate the simple things in life, and she was teaching everyone around her.

Brian was able to come to Jacksonville several times during weekends. My mom took care of Lauren so we could go out on a date and spend a little time together. Having dinner by the waterfront became a source of healing for us, as the Holy Spirit blew the fresh wind across our faces. Our marriage was strong, we were enduring.

CHAPTER 12

"Trust in the Lord with all your heart and lean not on your own understanding." Proverbs 3:5 NIV.

By the time we got down to eight remaining radiation treatments and 12 days until Go Home Day, the end of Jacksonville was in sight. We started packing up the apartment and sending moving boxes home with visiting family and friends. Lauren began making plans for when she returned home, but in the back of my mind, I couldn't help but be aware that we were far from done. Week 11 of chemo meant that we were only 21% through the entire treatment schedule.

Our apartment in Jacksonville was located downtown. Living in a neighborhood for eight weeks where many homeless men and women congregated was a constant reminder of how vast the need is for God's people to show His love. My child was fighting cancer, but we were fighting with the best medicine in a clean hospital. We had not missed a meal, we had a roof over our heads, and we were able to enjoy some good times in the city. But there were so many people around us who did not have guaranteed meals or a place to sleep at night. Whatever our struggles may be, we all have them. Whether it be cancer, depression, addiction, homelessness, we all struggle and need God's love.

One night, when I was feeling overwhelmed and anxious, Lauren asked me what was wrong. I explained how I was feeling and asked her how she handled those feelings. She said, "Well I'm a kid, so you can't take my advice."

Curious, I asked, "What is your 'kid' advice?"

Her response was brilliant. "Scream, cry, and hug my mommy!" After a giggle, she looked at me and said, "Seriously though, mommy, when I don't know what to do I just trust God. Everything has worked out okay so far, so it seems to be working." How does such a small child have so much wisdom?

The remaining days in Jacksonville were relatively smooth. Lauren was hospitalized once more for fever, but she recovered and was able to spend the last three days at the apartment. The radiation oncologist reassured us that she was very happy with how Lauren's treatments had gone, and that she wanted to see us back in six months, one year, and then every year for a while. Once again, she explained the possible long-term side effects of radiation—stroke, memory loss, learning disabilities—and said these may take a few years to show up. I didn't really pay much attention to what could happen to Lauren's health because of side effects. We had finished radiation, and that was all I could handle at the time. I'd worry about the next few years if God allowed us to get that far.

Finally, the last day of radiation came, July 2, 2014. Lauren handled it with grace and ease, and came out of the therapy room like a champion walking the victory lap. She held her radiation mask high and smiled as bright as the sun. We celebrated in the lobby with cookie cake, and she was able to ring the large bell hanging that signified end of treatment. Everyone clapped, and we were so thrilled to finally be through this phase of the journey. Finally, we could go home.

On July 3, 2014, after a long drive back to Atlanta and a warm welcome from our friends and neighbors, we *rested*. I mean, we rested. I slept about 16 hours a day for the next two days. Brian was beginning to worry, but I just told him that I needed to sleep off Jacksonville. It had taken a toll on my mind, body, and soul like nothing I'd ever experienced before. We celebrated the Fourth of July weekend with cookouts, boating, and sparklers. I took all three girls to see a movie. I remember looking over to my right and seeing all three girls sipping on slushies and chomping on candy and popcorn. My heart felt so full I thought it would burst. What joy these seemingly simple moments can bring, if only we take the time to see them.

CHAPTER 13

"Therefore, since we are surrounded by such a great cloud of witnesses, let us throw off everything that hinders and the sin that so easily entangles. And let us run with perseverance the race marked out for us" Hebrews 12:1 NIV.

I was so glad to be back among our friends and neighbors. The amount of support we received from the very moment we found out about Lauren's brain tumor was absolutely astonishing. Neighbors rallied together to notify Lauren's school, they helped to take care of our dog, the house, and the mail. Friends brought games and crafts to keep Audrey and Haley busy during surgery. They brought me a hairdryer so I could feel like a put-together person, even when living in a hospital. Gift cards and money started pouring in as people began to anticipate our needs. When we brought Lauren home from the hospital after surgery, neighbors and friends had decorated our living room for her with pretty sheets and balloons, along with a TV tray set up with crafts and goodies. A dinner schedule was organized and people brought meals to us on different nights each week. Friends would text me on their way to the grocery store to get my grocery list too.

And as we journeyed through, people continued to give and support us in so many ways. It would be nearly impossible for me to list every single one, especially since so many were anonymous, but there are some that stand out to me. Not that any one person or gift was more important than any other, but some of them were just so perfect in timing or need, or in God's answer to a specific prayer.

One of my favorite gifts to Lauren was a sheet that a church group had written Bible verses on and prayed over. With each hospitalization, I would lay that sheet over the foot of Lauren's bed at night and she and I would read the verses, thanking God for His promises and for literally covering us in His word.

Another particular gift that still brings me tears was a simple visit and Starbucks delivery from a neighbor of mine. It wasn't a planned visit, and it was well into the journey when it occurred, but one Saturday morning, during an unplanned hospital stay, my neighbor texted me and asked if I could use a coffee and a visit from a friend. Feeling especially down that day, I said yes, and she was there in about an hour. It was a sweet, quiet visit, nothing profound, but I knew that she was perfectly placed in that time and space by God and His omniscient way of knowing what my heart needed that day.

There were so many people who steadily supported us through the years of treatment. My next-door neighbor, whose family practically sacrificed their lives for supporting ours, would text me every night to tell me goodnight and that she loved me. In fact, I still get nightly messages to this day, and it's such a great reminder that someone is thinking of me.

One of my dearest friends form high school would occasionally send me a text with a quote, prayer, or bible verse. Sometimes all it said was "I love you." But again, because of the pertinence in timing or content, I knew that her words were directly given through her from God. They were always so perfect. Something

Chapter 13

about having an angel in my ear, directly in tune to God's voice, whispering in mine, was so intimate and comforting. Even though I've only seen her a handful of times in the last several years, and then for only a short time, she is the most precious friend I have. I feel as though she is a gift directly from my Abba Father to feed my soul.

There is one other person whose consistent encouragement was profound for me. One of my youth group leaders would send me messages through Facebook and through Lauren's blog. While many other people also did this, there was just something about his words, comments, and timing that let me know they were straight from God Himself. I don't know how you ever thank someone for that, but I know that these people were used as a vessel by God to deliver messages and hope to me during dark times.

Haley's mom was also a major supporter. Aside from taking Audrey in on a regular basis, she organized a huge event where people from all over the world sent Lauren stuffed animals (her favorite!) that represented where they lived. She received over 200 stuffed animals, which were a beautiful sign of love and encouragement from all around the world.

Of course there are so many other people who God used to sprinkle words of encouragement and hope, as well as to meet many practical needs for us along the way. Neighborhood and school fundraisers, church and community prayer partners, friends from every season of our lives . . . all were so special to us. God promised us a great cloud of witnesses, and we certainly were blessed to receive that promise.

CHAPTER 14

"She is clothed with strength and dignity; she can laugh at the days to come" Proverbs 31:25 NIV.

With summer coming to an end, Jacksonville behind us and our energy restored, we hit the ground running. Appointments, tests, blood transfusions, and chemotherapy didn't pause for celebration, so it was onward for us. The biggest hurdle was behind us though, and we knew that we could soldier through what was left to conquer.

Our world had stopped on March 11 so that we could focus on Lauren's treatment, but the rest of the world, which had kept on spinning, caught up to us when we got back from Jacksonville. The calendar in the "Learning Lab," the room in our house where the girls did all their homework, was still showing a March date, and now we turned it to July. School supplies were gathered, laundry piled high, and a new normal routine began to take shape, one that included IV fluids, G-tube meds, physical therapy, occupational therapy, and oncology appointments. We were starting to get the hang of the rhythm of life with cancer. Fortunately or unfortunately—I'm not sure which—cancer became a *part of* our lives more than a *disruption from* our lives.

For the first time in 14 weeks, Lauren didn't have to undergo any treatment or procedure until July 22, which was still weeks away. Her labs were great, no transfusions were needed, and she felt well enough to do more than sleep for once. It was the only time in her treatment that we would be able to avoid the "10 days after chemo" hospital admission for fever and low counts. We clung to that brief space of time so dearly. Her strength was slowly returning, and her mental toughness was off the charts. Chemotherapy was going fairly well. There was even a possibility of being able to do future treatments in the clinic and not having to stay overnight at the hospital anymore. Lauren was working diligently in her therapies to improve her strength, especially in her wrists, arms, and legs.

Lauren was given the opportunity on August 1 to interview with Neil Bortz, a radio celebrity, to talk about childhood cancer as part of the Care-a-Thon to raise money for the AFLAC Cancer Center. Lauren kept saying she was nervous to talk on the radio, but at the same time she wanted to share her story, she just didn't know what to say. The radio station had set up a live broadcast in the oncology clinic. After the day's chemotherapy, Lauren's nurse gave us permission to take her from the hospital over to the medical office building on the same campus for the interview. When her radio time came we were led into a room with two radio celebrities. We were asked a few questions and given the opportunity to share her story. The whole process was quick, 15 minutes tops, but it was one of what would become a number of opportunities to raise awareness and funds for this awful disease.

On July 22, a new chemotherapy medicine was introduced to Lauren's body. The drug was known to cause weakening of the heart muscles, so we had to watch closely for that, but Lauren's heart withstood the test. I truly believe her heart remained strong because Jesus Christ lives there and nothing can penetrate. She tolerated the new drug with minimal side effects. Then, slowly over the next few days, her body started to show signs of acute illness. Her heart rate began to creep up steadily over the next few days. She wasn't showing any other symptoms, so we decided to just keep a watch on it for a while. We ended up being discharged and going home even though she felt pretty yucky, but we all felt like that was to be expected.

I had to take a business trip to San Antonio, Texas in early August. I did not want to be away from Lauren or my family for that long, but to be honest I was kind of looking forward to a break. I had a quiet flight and my own hotel room. I knew that it would do my mind and heart a little good to be alone and to rest.

While I was gone Lauren developed a fever of 103 and we knew something just wasn't right. She had often developed a fever when her counts dropped in a predictable pattern, but it wasn't the right timeframe for her counts to be low. My mom, who was staying at the house to help with Lauren, took her to the emergency room to get lab work. The doctors decided to admit her to the hospital.

Unfortunately or fortunately—again I don't know which—we had a quick answer. Lauren had sepsis, which is a life-threatening infection in the blood. As a nurse, I knew that this would eventually happen to her, but as a mom, I had been optimistic that maybe, just maybe, we could avoid it. Lauren's blood cultures quickly showed positive results, so she was admitted for antibiotics and monitoring. Her blood pressure was slowly dropping, and her heart rate and fever were very high, so her doctor (an amazing and wonderful oncologist) decided to move her to the PICU for closer monitoring.

Anchors for Hope

As always, God's provision is perfect. He knew that this mommy's heart would be aching from so many miles away, and that knowing my baby was in the hands of my dear PICU friends would put my mind at ease. Lauren recovered well. Her heart rate came down along with her fever and the blood pressure improved. Of course, whenever I talked to her on the phone and asked her how she was doing she would say, "Mommy I'm great!"

Despite the stress of those few weeks Lauren was recognized as Youth of the Month by the optimist club and was given the opportunity to share her story. Her radio debut on the Care-a-Thon with Neil Bortz went well and they raised $1.6 million for the Aflac Cancer and Blood Disorders Center. Lauren found out she got the fifth-grade teacher she had been hoping for and school was about to begin.

CHAPTER 15

"The thief comes only to steal, kill and destroy. I have come that they may have life and have it to the full." John 10:10 NIV.

By late August we were really starting to feel the weight of this burden that was on us as a family. Our home was always full of people, medical staff, helpers, and family. One day, after Brian's 90-minute commute from work, he pulled onto our street and was stunned by a multitude of cars in the driveway. In our home at that time were Lauren's nurse, a delivery person with medical supplies, another delivery person with IV fluids, and someone bringing dinner. Brian sat in his car in front of our house for 45 minutes, completely overtaken by how cancer had consumed our home.

We had started to encounter many difficulties that our new normal presented to us. I had a four-door family sedan, and we weren't able to fit her wheelchair and all of her equipment in it. Brian and I would have to trade cars or split the family and take both vehicles wherever we went. Sometimes I would just have to forgo the wheelchair and carry Lauren, which was very difficult.

Just when we were sinking into desperation and isolation, our neighborhood rallied around us in an amazing and loving way. They put together a humongous tennis benefit, which they called "Love for Lauren," and they pulled in community sponsors to donate food and raffle items, and tennis pros to play a round robin tournament for everyone to watch. So many people from her school and from all over the Atlanta area came to show support for Lauren. It was absolutely amazing. The money they raised allowed us to buy a vehicle that would hold Lauren's equipment and wheelchair. The new, larger vehicle was a huge blessing to us, but even more so was seeing all of the people who came out to support her, love her, and be there for us. During that weekend we were shown in a powerful way that we weren't going at it alone. To see our neighbors and friends rally around us in such a big way was just kind of a pat on the back, as if to say, "We got this, we're in this together, and we're still here for you."

Lauren was in the hospital during the tennis benefit, but we were able to FaceTime her. Some of the Atlanta Hawks cheerleaders that had been at the basketball game with her a few months earlier came out to the tennis event, and they were sweet and kind enough to FaceTime Lauren. Even when she was in the hospital, everyone went above and beyond to make her feel special and loved.

We were six months in by this point, and friends and neighbors were still providing meals and help for us on a regular basis. On August 12, God allowed us the joy of another clear MRI. We were all so excited and so thankful. I wish I had video of the moment Lauren and I shared when we were talking about it, because it was so real and powerful, but I can only paraphrase.

Chapter 15

Lauren said, "Mommy, you know how people say 'actions speak louder than words?' Well, I think that explains why God let this happen to me. God didn't give me cancer, because it's evil and He is good, but He let me have cancer so He can show me how much He loves me and takes care of me. If I just read the Bible and go to church, I just know the words, but because I have cancer, God can show me His actions of how He loves me."

It's no wonder Jesus has such a tender heart for children. They see Him so clearly.

Love seemed to be pouring over us, from all sides. On August 17, our dear friend and neighbor hosted a Paint It Forward fundraiser event for Lauren at her art studio. Friends, family members, and even strangers came out to paint with us. Lauren chose a picture of a bird as the class painting, and the teacher donated her completed painting to Lauren. The picture still hangs in Lauren's closet, along with a canvas on which each participant had placed a painted handprint as a sign of support. It was such a fun time because Lauren loves to paint and craft and she was able to do it with all of her closest friends. She was momentarily free from pumps and IVs, and was able to just be a kid for the afternoon. We are so thankful for our friend for donating to us this special event and for putting a smile on Lauren's face.

By the end of August, Lauren was feeling well enough to visit her fifth-grade class. Lauren was continuing to manage her treatments, but the in and out of the hospital stays was starting to wear on her. Even though she would only show a smile, my sweet girl was getting tired and frustrated. She missed her sisters. She missed school. She missed normal, even though she could hardly remember it. She did everything she was supposed to do.

She took all of her medicines, knew all of her treatment plans, did physical therapy, did occupational therapy, and followed her doctors' orders. She kept getting knocked down, but she had proven that she was a fighter, and she refused to give up. She had downloaded "Eye of the Tiger" from Rocky onto her iPad, and listened to the song frequently for inspiration.

By September, I started to feel like a broken record. Hospital, home. Hospital, home. I can only imagine how tired everyone must have been from seeing the words repeat over and over on the blog that I had started to keep friends and family updated on her treatments. I was certainly tired of writing them. Even on our best days, I could see the bigger picture of a steady decline in endurance, energy, and strength. I think one of the hardest angles of the cancer journey for all of us to cope with was the long-term unanswered questions. We didn't know which side effects would go away and which ones would be permanent. We didn't know if any of the therapy would allow her to walk normally again or if she would always be a little slow and weak. We didn't know if her crooked little fingers would ever straighten out, or if her hearing damage would ever abate or only worsen. So many unknowns, so much to adapt to.

It was also hard to watch more and more of Lauren's innocence being stripped away. Gifts no longer mattered, she just wanted to be well. What the other girls saw as chores Lauren saw as activities she could no longer do, but wished that she could. She did her Algebra homework with a smile because she was so happy to be doing something normal. She would even take tests during chemotherapy so as not to get behind. It was something that other kids were doing, and that was all she wanted—to be normal.

Chapter 15

But cancer took away any chance of living a normal life from Lauren. Our old sense of normal was stolen away in a heartbeat, but the new normal trickled in little by little. For an entire year she could not take showers or baths because of the lines and tubes coming out of her body. Only sponge baths were acceptable. Her nurses helped us battle this loss. Each week, her port had to be re-accessed, which is like having to start a new IV every week, only the needle is much bigger and it goes in your chest. When Lauren was hospitalized during the time to have her port re-accessed, the nurse would take out the old line and give her a 30-minute break before inserting the new one. During this time, we would lay pillows in the tub and fill it up enough for her to lay back and relax, or lay on her tummy and pretend to swim. It was a glimmer of normal, and we were grateful for it.

School went on without her. Although she kept up with assignments through homebound instruction, she missed out on events and daily interaction with friends. She lost touch with trends, popular toys, and sayings and fashion. She didn't keep up with who liked whom.

Most of all, cancer stole her innocence, her naivety, her youth. She had no routine of school, sports, and home for dinner. She lost the ability to be carefree. She lost energy, strength, physical functions. She lost her independence from me.

Truly, cancer stole from all of us. As a family, we lost vacations, evenings around the dinner table, and an entire summer. As a mother of two other girls, I lost the tween years and the transition from elementary to middle school with Audrey and Haley. I lost a lot of my ability to feel. I grew accustomed to blocking emotions, pushing them aside to focus on tasks. I lost my ability to tap into processing and understand my emotions and feelings. I lost the sense of organized home management, cleaning schedules, and meal planning. I lost alone time with Brian. I lost celebrating for my brother as he welcomed his daughter. I lost the opportunity to teach Lauren about normal female growth and development. I lost the ability to be away from Lauren without constant worry, and to take a headache at face value. I lost the ability to establish routines, norms, and patterns in our life and home.

Our whole family had to adjust to these losses and the side effects. Since Lauren experienced hearing pain and anxiety, especially in crowded places, we had to start carrying headphones everywhere to help block the noise. Her eyes changed frequently, so she had constant changes in her prescription glasses, and the frequent weight change meant the glasses never fit right. We came to love bald heads, the feel of that soft, sweet fuzz. Lauren and her sisters even made a YouTube video called "I Like Bald Heads" to the tune of a popular Sir Mix-a-Lot song.

Sleepless nights became routine. Preparing her medications every morning and night took 30 minutes minimum, and Brian and I would have a conversation every night about who would go to the emergency room if the need came about. Our marriage, though strong, had become a medical management partnership. Fevers and blood transfusions could be predicted almost to the day. Low blood counts and clinic visits were routine. My purse no longer held gum and nail files, but instead held a thermometer, numbing cream, and cling wrap for her port. Suitcases were always packed and ready for an ambulance ride or hospital stay, and Audrey and Haley had become packing experts.

Chapter 15

One night, we had a handyman doing some repairs at our house when Lauren developed a fever, and I had to take her to the emergency room. I'll never forget his deer-in-the-headlights look as he watched us calmly call the emergency room and load her in the car, while talking about the logistics of the next day.

Stares from strangers no longer fazed us either. Lauren would wave at someone who was looking at her curiously, offer a big smile, and say, "Hi, I'm Lauren, and I have cancer!" Chemotherapy side effects were new every day, and nothing surprised us after a few months of treatment. Seeing Lauren's face on a pamphlet or billboard as the face of childhood cancer became routine, although the sting never completely disappeared. She was learning to embrace her life as it was.

Lauren learned to accept the droopy eye that treatment had left her with. She constantly struggled to find food that tasted decent to her ever-changing taste buds. Lauren says that she can't even remember herself before cancer, and to a degree it is hard to even remember what our normal used to be.

And yet, Lauren's optimism was always at the ready. Here's one post that she wrote on October 18, 2015, on the blog that kept family and friends updated on her treatment:

"Hi this is Lauren so if I mess up well I am a sixth grader. I thought I'd try writing a blog I know my mom is best at this though. The other day we were passing the fair and my mom and step dad (I think of him more as just another dad) made a joke about putting me in the rodeo and letting me ride a bull. I said I think over the past year I've been on a mental bull ride. I'll explain what I mean in a second. You guys have heard about all the treatment and the pain and all that jazz you may think that's tough but it's nothing

compared to the toughest part of cancer THE MENTAL PART. Especially as a kid you have to worry about adult stuff like what's my blood pressure, did I get all my meds, when are my doctors' appointments? Also there are feelings that come with it (hormones don't help) I remember times when I was laying in the hospital bed and I'd tell mommy I just need to cry I feel really sad but I don't know why. Sometimes I felt really scared sometimes I would say God just take me now but now I see that God has used me to share joy and love and I'm glad that he chose me to share those things. There are medicines and therapy session that have helped me with my feelings and lots of little tricks like here is something a lot of should do when you feel stressed or anxious make a list of things that make you feel happy. Ok going back to how God chose me to take this journey I have a verse I'd like to share Proverbs 3:5 trust in the Lord with all your heart do not lean on your own understanding. I've learned to trust him with whatever he puts me through. Now what you've all been waiting for an update I have been having a lot of g-tube pain plus I am on steroids which we are weaning off of. My anxiety is much better I haven't had any more shakes. We are done with avaston. That should be it. Bye."

Every time I read this post, I'm reminded of the heavy burden that has been placed on this young girl's heart, and the strength that God has given her to carry it.

CHAPTER 16

"For we live by faith, not by sight" 2 Corinthians 5:7 NIV.

We all craved normal, but we were constantly reminded how not normal we were, even when people were reaching out to help us. About six months into chemotherapy, halfway through, I was invited to the Quiet Heroes Banquet in September of 2014, a local event that honors mothers of children with cancer. I had no idea what to expect, and I'm not even sure why I ended up going to be honest. I don't usually enjoy going to things alone. But I was curious, so I decided to attend.

I drove down to the fancy Buckhead hotel, went up into the lobby, and found my name badge. The greeters handed me a swag bag that was overwhelmingly generous. I couldn't believe how much people had donated for the attendees, and it was all for moms. It was such a refresher to have a little bit of fun and me stuff. The bag was full to the top: lotions, lipstick, candles, jewelry, a t-shirt, socks . . . so many great things!

They had a large auction, and as I walked around, I saw hundreds of items to raise money for CURE Childhood Cancer, a nonprofit organization dedicated to raising money for childhood cancer research. Many sports celebrities had donated autographed pictures, footballs, baseballs, and cleats. There were trips and luggage, purses and jewelry, and so many more things to bid on. When we went into the dining hall, we sat down at beautifully decorated tables with random seating assignments, and I couldn't have picked two more opposite women to sit between.

The woman sitting to my left had just lost her child to cancer within the last few months. The woman to my right was a pro at cancer events. She had been doing this for a long time, so it was nothing new for her and seemed like no big deal. And there I was, somewhere in the middle. I teared up when they showed Lauren's picture on the screen, and I found myself terrified that I was going to become like either of the women to my left or right. I honestly didn't want to be either. I didn't want to be the woman on the left to have lost her child and felt the hole that was undoubtedly left in her heart. I could not imagine having to bear that pain. But I also didn't want to be the woman on my right, the woman who had been doing this so long that it had become comfortable—just a part of normal life. I was scared because I knew that I was going to fall into one of those two categories, although I had no idea which one. I was scared to death about both.

Shortly after the Quiet Heroes banquet, we went to a place called Camp Sunshine at Camp Twin Lakes in October of 2014. Camp Twin Lakes is a camp location that hosts a variety of events for special groups. Camp Sunshine is the name of the camps for kids with cancer and their siblings and families. We went for Family Camp, which is a weekend event where families of kids with cancer all come together to have fun and build a community of support.

Chapter 16

We had an amazing time getting to know other families. It felt so good to be in a place where carrying a syringe of meds in your pocket wasn't weird, and everybody understood your form of tired. But it also felt so sad to be sitting around a campfire sharing s'mores with so many families who were journeying through childhood cancer. I found myself upset because I did not want to be a part of this community. Don't get me wrong, it's the most supportive, amazing community you will ever find, but no one chooses to become part of it.

Just how much our life had truly changed because of cancer really hit home when we left the camp. Lauren had developed an infection around her feeding tube. Because the camp is so awesome, they have an oncologist from our hospital on staff at all times, so we were able to see the doctor, and she recommended going to the ER. Whereas normal families would have rushed off to the ER immediately, we cleaned up our cabin, had breakfast in the mess hall, and then loaded the car and headed to the hospital, stopping at the gas station for bubble gum and candy. Then we turned up the radio, sang our favorite songs as loud as we could and headed to the emergency room, everyone in a great mood. That's childhood cancer for you. A trip to the emergency room is part of normal.

We were figuring out how to roll from one context to the next, from home to the hospital, to a cancer-related event or trip. Our most elaborate trip came from the Make-A-Wish Foundation. From the very beginning of Lauren's diagnosis, the social worker at the hospital told us that she had been nominated for Make-A-Wish. We honestly really didn't give any thought to it because we just needed to focus on treatment, but eventually the volunteers came to our house. They met with Lauren and talked to her about what her wish was, asking if she knew what she wanted or if she needed some ideas of what other kids had done. She knew exactly what she wanted. She wanted something that the whole family could enjoy, that we could all do together. So she chose to have us go on a Disney cruise.

We knew that her health had to be just right for us to go, and in those early days, her reactions to treatment were so unpredictable. She would feel great one day and horrible the next, so we told them we really needed to wait until late summer or early fall because by then she should be done with treatment. She should be feeling somewhat stronger and then hopefully she would be able to really enjoy the trip. So we prayed and begged and pleaded with God to get us to the point of going on the trip, and then put it in the back of our minds.

CHAPTER 17

"Today in the town of David a Saviour has been born to you; he is the Messiah, the Lord" Luke 2:11 NIV.

When we weren't at the hospital or a cancer-related event, we tried to find some sense of our forgotten normalcy. Lauren had been asking to go to the park for a few weeks, so we got up early on a Sunday morning before it was too hot outside. After 15 minutes of sitting on a swing (not even swinging, just sitting) she was wiped out and wanted to go home. Watching her at the park was so painful because she just kept looking around at all the kids who could climb rock walls and slide on slides, and yes hopefully she would one day be able to do those things again, but right then, in the thick of it, she was tired. Her body was worn out. She still showed a constant smile, but asked about giving up and said over and over again that this journey was so hard.

She wanted to be able to swim and shower, to take out the garbage and clean the kitchen. She wanted to be able to walk freely around the house without having to wait for someone to help her down the stairs or push her IV pole. She wanted to be able to go out without being completely exhausted from just getting ready. She wanted normal.

Yet most of her days were spent at Children's Healthcare of Atlanta (CHOA). If I had to choose a hospital though, I could not have asked God for a better one to treat my child. I first came to know of CHOA when I moved to Atlanta in 2008. I had been a Pediatric ICU nurse since graduation from nursing school in Tennessee, so it only made sense that I would continue that career when I moved. I began working in the PICU at the Scottish Rite campus of CHOA, the one closest to our home. The people were amazing to work with, and the hospital system easily earns its title as one of Atlanta's best places to work.

The daily grind of night shifts coupled with the constant emotional drain of taking care of critically ill children took its toll on me, so eventually I moved on to other nursing roles. But during my time at Scottish Rite, I learned a great deal about the hospital and its core values and operations, and I met many amazing people. Many of those friendships continued even after my departure. Little did I know they would become valuable on a whole new level five years after I left. I had known the place as my work, but now it would become my second home—from the chapel, where I spent countless hours crying and praying, sitting in silence, in fear, in disbelief, to the chaplain who would pray in our room day after day, standing by Lauren's side as she described her vision of Jesus calling her to Him.

We were lucky in that the hospital was only a 40-minute drive from our home. Some families we met traveled hours, I mean six, seven, eight hours, just to receive treatment there.

Food became a big part of our stay at CHOA. The cafeteria food was pretty good, especially at lunchtime. There is a good deal of variety in choice, so eating there day after day was bearable. One of the chefs took special care of Lauren, making special requests for her and delivering them to her room himself

Chapter 17

on occasion. He hosted a special cooking class to let the kids make strawberry shortcakes one day, which Lauren loved. We spent many late nights searching the vending machines for whatever might taste good to Lauren's chemo taste buds, which got pretty interesting. I remember one night when she got White Castle burgers, pineapple orange Jell-O, and a bottle of Yoo-hoo chocolate milk. I sat by her bedside thinking "I can't believe I'm letting my kid eat this!" but I was just so happy to see her eating at that point that I let it slide.

Another amazing treat at CHOA is the therapy dogs. There are multiple dogs that work at CHOA, visiting children and helping calm fears and anxiety. These dogs became so powerful for Lauren that her doctors ended up recommending a service dog of her own.

The child life specialists play one of the most vital roles in the hospital staffing. Their job is to work with the children, siblings, and families to educate them about the illness, diagnoses, treatments, and hospital happenings. They help encourage and entertain the patients and siblings, while providing support during treatments, pain management, and even death. They are absolutely incredible, providing the glue that pulls all of the other pieces of a stay at CHOA together into one cohesive, doable, puzzle. They had such an impact on Lauren that she now wants to become a child life specialist when she grows up.

When you become a "frequent flyer" in the hospital, you start to find comfort within those walls. "Hotel CHOA" as we came to call it, was home away from home. Most of the time, when you enter, you are just hoping and praying that you will be able to leave in better shape than you came, but the comfort of knowing that these people have got your back is so welcoming in tough times.

Knowing that they will celebrate with you in big and little successes makes them like family.

They become family because they are there with you day in and day out, in the best and worst parts of the journey. They laugh with you, cry with you, drop to their knees in prayer with you. They even made Lauren a hospital staff badge of her own. When you just can't parent anymore because you're too tired, overwhelmed, or distraught, they will step in and fulfill your child's needs while still finding some way to fulfill yours too. Over time you find your favorite hospital room. In Aflac, we lovingly call this room "the penthouse." It is in the back of the unit, away from the hustle and bustle of the nurses' station and doors, and its location provides for extra square footage. To outsiders, this may sound excessive or greedy, but when you spent 80 – 90% of your year in a hospital you want a room you can live in. The Starbucks and gift shop in the lobby became like a refuge, practical places to find comfort and cope with stress.

We were frequently reminded of just how blessed we were by the hospital's facilities and staff. Each time Lauren was admitted to the Aflac unit, the nurses would have her room set up just how she liked it. Pretty pillow case and blanket on the bed and the blue IV pole that kept all the power cords organized. One night a nurse even brought Taco Bell in for Lauren because she knew she had been craving it. They never let us down.

We were not sure what to expect when we learned that Lauren's treatment schedule would have her continue chemotherapy over the Thanksgiving and Christmas holidays, including the 24th and 25th. We had already endured every holiday in the hospital up to that point, but Christmas in the hospital was strange. The hospital does an amazing job of making you feel as cozy as possible. The donors and volunteers pour love and encouragement into the kids who are in the hospital on Christmas. Santa came in several nights in a row and brought gifts. He delivered a huge bag of presents on Christmas Eve for Lauren that were so specific to her and her wishes and her likes that we were deeply touched at how the hospital took extra effort in making sure that this was the best Christmas that she could have, despite the fact that she wasn't at home.

Even though Lauren was in the hospital over Christmas, she had a strong desire to help another cancer family. CURE Childhood Cancer had asked Lauren to make a wish list so that a donor could give Christmas gifts to her and our family, but she politely declined and asked if she could be a donor instead. She told them that her family and friends were taking great care of her and that she wanted someone else to be blessed, so she designed a t-shirt to sell, and raised over $700 to provide Christmas gifts and household items to another childhood cancer family at our hospital. She had such a great time shopping online and being a Secret Santa.

Her school rallied again for Lauren during December. Each student in every grade wrote notes on papers, cut the paper into a lightbulb shape, and hung them around the room like Christmas lights. Then each class in the entire school took on different projects to decorate Lauren's hospital room. They made candle jars to light in the room to give it that candlelit feeling. Teachers came and hung Christmas lights in her room. They made a Christmas wreath, decorated the window to look like it had snowed, and decorated her hospital room door like a snowman. Even the bathroom was decked out with Christmas lights. The school nurse put together a makeshift fireplace and chimney with cardboard boxes so Lauren could hang a stocking in her room. The entire school came together to let Lauren know that they were thinking of her. Their creativity and love made Christmas a special time for her, despite the fact that she was undergoing chemotherapy that day.

It was a strange feeling for me to be on the receiving end of so much generosity that Christmas. I have always been a giving person, and I truly enjoy knowing that someone else will receive joy, happiness, and met needs when I give. I love helping with Angel Trees at Christmas, buying groceries for families in need, and giving in special circumstances.

Every year on Christmas Eve since Brian and I have been married, we have made it a tradition to light a candle for each person our family has helped throughout that year. We started this tradition as a way to help the girls have a visual demonstration to help them understand how we spread God's light by helping others. This was especially effective when they were young, and has continued to be a very special tradition for us. We would light the candles, then pray for the people we were blessed to be able to help. We would also explain to the girls that at any point in our lives we could become the family in need. We thanked God for allowing us to be the givers for another year.

When Christmas came that year, we found ourselves on the receiving side. We had been abundantly blessed, and learning to gracefully receive from others became a humbling learning experience for us all. How could you ever fully express your gratitude when someone gives to you, especially when you could technically find a way to take care of yourself, but others want to make it easier? How do you set aside the pride of taking care of your own needs, and just graciously accept the generosity of others? I learned that God uses those opportunities, not just to bless the receiver, but to bless the giver as well.

Chapter 17

So many people had the opportunity to experience the joy of giving by giving to us that year.

And when the time came for us to light the candles, God provided a beautiful visual for our girls. You see, we didn't light many candles that year, very few compared to our usual, but we lit one large candle for all of the many people who had given to us. We were given the opportunity to pray for the givers, to thank God for their blessings and for their generosity, and for loving us in every position we found ourselves. We thanked Him for providing for us through the givers, and we taught the girls to never take for granted the opportunity to give when you have it. And He taught us also, that when people give you gifts that you might think you don't need, it may be because He wants to increase your ability to pay it forward to others in need.

The Christmas holiday was really put into perspective for us that year about what really mattered. Jesus Christ came to save us and give us hope, and family is more important than anything else. We didn't have a Christmas tree or decorations up at our house for Christmas, but Christmas came anyway. We saw more Santa Clauses than anyone could ever imagine, and not a single one of them could deliver healing or a cure for cancer, but on the 25th, God's perfect gift still remained and the hope of Christ was still present. An opportunity to spend a quiet evening with our entire family at home a few days before Christmas was more precious to us than anything that could be wrapped in pretty paper and bows. Not the Grinch, not the Devil, not even cancer could take away our salvation, and for that we were thankful beyond words.

CHAPTER 18

"We have this hope as an anchor for the soul, firm and secure" Hebrews 6:19 NIV.

The month of March 2015 was a big month for Lauren. She celebrated her 11th birthday and recognized a full year since being diagnosed with cancer. Since early in Lauren's diagnosis, the therapy dogs at CHOA played a big part in calming her and making her smile. As chemotherapy started to take its toll on her body, we seriously considered getting a service dog for her. We really didn't know exactly what she would need, and the timing never seemed right. We gathered information, asked questions, and did some research, but nothing seemed to drive us forward.

We ended up spending a lot of time with our neighbor's dog Lexi, because she was such a calming influence for Lauren. We talked a little with our neighbor about getting info from her breeder in case we decided to get Lauren a dog at some point, but nothing serious. Then, in January of 2015, our neighbor told me that the breeder had a new litter. Still, we had at least four months to go with treatment, and Lauren seemed to be getting worse, so we just weren't ready to commit.

Anchors for Hope

At one of Lauren's clinic appointments, Lauren met a young man who was at the clinic for his last day of chemotherapy. He asked my mom, who was with Lauren that day, for my contact information. Mom wasn't sure if she should give my number to a stranger, but decided that he was part of the Aflac family and seemed to have a good motive, so she did. The next day I got a call from that sweet young man, telling me about an amazing organization called Team Summer, that allows kids with cancer to surprise each other with a special gift, just for fun, and he had nominated Lauren. He told me to start thinking about what she might like, and that it could be a need, but also had to be something fun that she wanted that would help her cope. He suggested things like an iPad, gaming system, headphones, etc. I told him I'd have to think about it.

I got a message from my neighbor later that afternoon telling me that the breeder's puppies would be ready in March, but that there were only a few left, so if I was thinking about getting one I needed to act soon. I felt right then that God had given me the answer. God had provided the sign. I told her to tell the breeder to hold one for us. We still weren't 100% sure that this was exactly it, but I knew that God was up to something.

Shortly thereafter, Lauren's doctors called a care team conference to discuss Lauren's worsening anxiety and to brainstorm ways to cope. Lauren's oncologist and psychiatrist highly recommended a service dog who could intervene in anxiety and panic attacks and who could also provide seizure alert for us. God's confirmation was clear at that point.

I called the director for Team Summer, told her the whole puppy story, and said that we knew for sure what Lauren's gift should be.

Chapter 18

She was thrilled, knowing that her daughter Summer had been had found comfort in a kitten throughout her own cancer journey. The planning began.

Knowing Lauren, I knew that she would want to name her puppy, but as part of the service dog training the puppy would need to begin hearing its name before coming home. So we concocted a story and told Lauren that the breeder was so inspired by her that she wanted her to name the last two puppies. We showed her a picture of one brown and white pup and one black with hints of white. Lauren thought for a minute, pointed to the brown and white one, and said, "I think she should be called Lilly." Then I asked her about the black one—which we had already picked for her—and she said without hesitation, "Her name is Hope!"

I thought to myself, "Hello, Lord, thank you for being so present!" These are the kinds of signs that people miss in their daily lives if they aren't seeking Jesus.

After speaking with several other "momcologists" whose children had service animals, I connected with a private trainer to set up service dog training. Through the generous fundraisers that have been done in Lauren's honor we were able to cover part of this training.

My dad and I drove to Lexington, Kentucky on a Saturday in March to pick up this precious "Hope." My heart was so full! God's provision is glorious, His love for us overflowing!

The big day finally arrived. Team Summer gifts are always a surprise, so Lauren had no idea what was coming. It is not an exaggeration to say that it was love at first sight, an instant bond between Lauren and Hope. It was almost as if the puppy knew she had a special mission in this world. A mission to help a little girl bear all that she must. Lauren was overheard whispering in the puppy's ear, "You are just a bundle of Hope."

Hope immediately began training as a service dog. That meant that Hope could go everywhere with Lauren, so instead of crying and screaming during medical procedures, Lauren would sit calmly with Hope on her lap. Instead of staying isolated in her room at the hospital, Lauren began to go out in the halls to share Hope with other kids with cancer. In short, Lauren began to focus less on her own struggles and more on trying to help other kids sharing her battle.

The puppy, Hope, joined our family and was a huge support for Lauren throughout her treatment.

CHAPTER 19

"A furious squall came up, and the waves broke over the boat, so that it was nearly swamped" Mark 4:37 NIV.

We soon passed through winter and into spring, and on April 10, 2015, Lauren finally completed her schedule of chemotherapy. During Lauren's last chemotherapy hospitalization, I kept hearing three words whispered in my head, but was afraid to say them out loud for fear of jinxing the fact that this was the last chemo. For many childhood cancer patients the end of treatment is only temporary, and cancer eventually rears its ugly head again only to start the cycle over. The part of me that was a nurse and an educated "momcologist" was way too smart to say out loud, but for some reason the phrase just kept coming to mind.

"It is finished."

Day after day, throughout the entire week the phrase kept repeating itself in my head. And then it hit me, almost as if God said to me, "Hello! I'm trying to tell you something. IT IS FINISHED!"

It was finished when His Son died on the cross. Death was conquered, which means cancer and any other evil sinful thing in this world was conquered too. Yeah, maybe cancer will come back some time, or maybe it won't. Maybe Lauren will have some other new side effects, or maybe she won't. But none of that matters because regardless of what happens in this time, on this earth, it is finished. Christ finished the struggle when He died for us and set us free from sin and death. We have eternal life, and even if our entire earthly life is riddled with cancer, disease, strife of any kind, our eternal lives will be holy and pure, because IT IS FINISHED. Because my Jesus Christ paid it all.

"Therefore when Jesus had received the sour wine, He said, 'It is finished!' And He bowed His head and gave up His spirit." John 19:30

By the last week of April 2015, the time had come for another MRI, and Lauren was constantly showing me how to live in faith and perseverance. She had become fairly used to MRI scans, but some anxiety started to creep in around her port being accessed because it's such a huge needle that goes into her chest. She'd been trying to calm herself and prepping for this particular MRI. This was the first one off of treatment, so we were all a little on edge. When the time came to insert the giant needle, she didn't even flinch. Sometimes I would forget how mentally tough she had to be as a 10-year-old. She was then sedated and taken to the scanner. Her MRI lasted from approximately 3:15PM to 5:30PM. Brian had taken her, and he called me at 6:16PM to say they were on their way home. When Lauren's oncologist called at 6:30PM, I knew something was very wrong.

Lauren's MRI revealed a new spot in her brain, in the same area as her previous tumor. They thought this could be one of three things: radiation damage, chemotherapy effects from the

Chapter 19

chemo that was injected directly into her brain, or a new tumor. There were only two ways to find out, through surgery or to wait and watch. Based on the location, lab work, and Lauren's overall current physical assessment, her doctor felt like it was most likely radiation damage that we were seeing, and that it was not worth subjecting Lauren to another brain surgery to obtain a biopsy.

We decided to wait and watch for any new symptoms or changes. We would have another MRI in eight weeks. In the meantime we would discuss the MRI findings with Lauren's radiation oncologist when we went for a checkup in Jacksonville the next week. She would be able to give us her opinion on the spot location, while considering the radiation mapping of where exactly Lauren had had radiation. If the spot was radiation damage, her Jacksonville oncologist would know best where that damage was likely to show up.

I remember very vividly that we were concerned, but we were not afraid. God is the same yesterday, today, and forever. He had carried us this far, and He would carry us further. While we wondered what the radiation oncologist would see and say, we were not anxious. We strove to "walk by faith, not by sight" (2 Corinthians 5:7).

In my journal of that day, I wrote:

> *We are strong. We are more than conquerors, and we will continue to praise God and claim victory in His name! "No, in all these things we are more than conquerors through him who loved us" (Romans 8:37). "May the God of hope fill you with all joy and peace in believing, so that you will abound in hope by the power of the Holy Spirit" (Romans 15:13). Both cancer and Satan seem to think they can*

maintain a grip that will yield them victory. Both cancer and Satan seem oblivious to the fact that they are defeated EVERY DAY through prayer and the power of God.

Lauren had originally had a radiation follow-up scheduled for January 2015, but at that time she was too sick to travel. When I called to reschedule, they offered May 11, 2015. I said okay to this, not knowing anything about that date except that chemo should be done by then. But God knew the date. God's timing is perfect. God knew that in late April, a new area of concern would be revealed on MRI. God knew that this news would bring back the weight and the overshadowing cloud of seriousness and concern that was so fresh to us a year ago.

In that moment I felt myself entrenched in a spiritual battle, one that I knew God was winning. Cancer and Satan had laid plans for Lauren and me to travel to Jacksonville blind. Cancer and Satan hoped that we would naively go into a routine follow-up with the radiation oncologist and be surprised by the new concerning area in Lauren's brain. Cancer and Satan set the trip to be full of burden and fear.

But God said "No." God orchestrated our appointment date to be close enough to the MRI to give us peace of mind, and far enough from the MRI to prepare our minds to receive information. Between the MRI and the follow-up in Jacksonville, God gave us gorgeous weather for a weekend in Florida, and the people around us arranged a special trip for us. Thanks to family, friends, and a donation from a family member's travel agency, Lauren, Hope, and I spent two nights in Disney's All-Star Movies Resort. And thanks to God's beautiful timing, we were also spending time with some of our greatest prayer warriors and supporters, my brother and his family. They just *happened* to also be staying at the same resort that night.

Chapter 19

I sat by the Fantasia pool that night and cried happy tears while watching Lauren do flip after flip in the water. She swam under, she jumped in, and she splashed and played for the first time in over a year. She was not hooked up to any IVs or tubes, just her 10-year-old body in a swimsuit, and the smile on her face was indescribably glorious. And through God's grace and mercy, He gave this mommy's heart the joy and happiness that Satan and cancer had been trying so hard to steal.

After our short trip to Orlando, we made our way to Jacksonville and met with Lauren's radiation oncologist. Because she was the expert when it comes to proton therapy and radiation damage, we were hoping that she would tell us she felt certain the new spot on the MRI was radiation damage. But that is not what she said. Instead, she explained to us all the reasons why she did *not* think it was radiation damage, but most likely a new tumor. We weren't expecting that heavy blow.

We would find out more over the next few days, but we began anticipating more tests and possibly another surgery over the next week or two. Our friends, family, and entire communities were put on a prayer watch while we waited.

During that time, I truly believe that God heard the cries of so many people, the groans of our hearts. Lauren's physicians conducted a conference so that each doctor could give his or her perspective of the current situation. After everyone's medical expertise was laid on the table and compiled, the evidence suggested that the chances were much greater that this new spot was radiation damage, rather than a tumor. No one could say with 100% certainty, but we were grateful, and we trusted in the Lord. For that moment, we could relax. No more surgery! Lauren would have another MRI in four weeks, but until then, we celebrated every day of life and enjoyed God's goodness.

One day we took a boat ride, and Lauren was so excited to feel the wind blowing in the tiny fuzz of hair that had started growing back!

Through June, July, and August, we treated the new spot as radiation damage (necrosis), which meant that tissue had died from the radiation done a year before and caused swelling in her brain. This treatment also meant a new round of medications, which created problems of their own. The headaches and nausea diminished, but Lauren began to have severe G-tube pain, even more brittle bones then before, and delayed healing, which meant the fractures in her feet weren't going anywhere for months. We had to delay one of the brain swelling drugs to give her G-tube time to heal, but of course that meant that we were likely to see another rise in the symptoms from brain swelling, including headaches, double vision, and nausea. We were on a see-saw, and couldn't find the balance in the middle.

The longevity of this journey started to weigh on us. It had become routine for us to have challenges, doctors' appointments, and new meds. It had become so common in fact, that we couldn't really remember life before it. Doctors' appointments required hours of preparation, packing medications, portable feeding and IV pumps, changes of clothes, strollers, and snacks. Most of the time the information or treatment was so intense that only Brian, myself, or my mom could go. We found it constantly difficult to find a balance in all the ongoing medical problems and drugs, risk versus reward, and what was truly best for Lauren's quality of life. I felt like we were on a vicious cycle of constantly shifting problems. In fixing one problem, we would create another, and to fix that problem we would create a third, or use a drug that has unknown side effects, not enough research to know what it's going to do to her long-term. We were trying to help her in the present, even though we might be hurting her down the road. But did we even need to think about that, or should we just focus on giving her the opportunity to get down the road? All these things weighed on our minds daily. This type of parenting was harder than anything else we'd ever experienced. There is no instruction manual for this stuff.

Lauren returned to doing hospital homebound schooling because the energy and endurance needed to go to school every day became too much for her. She wanted to go, and missed her friends so much. She had two great days when she was able to go sit in her classroom like a normal kid, but those two days just weren't enough. Of course I'm stretching the word "normal." She went to school with a cast on one foot and a boot on the other, bald head, G-tube, and scars beyond imagination. I'm so thankful for that glimpse we had of health and normalcy, but I'm angry because it was so brief. Why did she only get two days of feeling good and getting to be a normal middle school kid?

But we hadn't lost hope. We knew, even then, that we were blessed by God's abundance, His love for us, and the family of Christ. We were just tired, that's all. But we pushed on. We wanted to keep fighting, keep smiling, and keep sharing the Hope of God with everyone we met.

Anchors for Hope

Lauren had a brief glimpse of what it would be like to return to school, like a normal kid. No matter what comes her way, she will always have a resilient spirit and the courage to smile in the face of great hardship.

Chapter 20

"He stilled the storm to a whisper; the waves of the sea were hushed" Psalm 107:29.

The fall of 2015 was full of fun activities. Finally, in September, the Make-A-Wish volunteers came out to our house again. They gave Lauren her wish and told her, "You're going on a Disney cruise!"

Audrey and Haley were surprised, and the volunteers had brought gifts for all of the girls, even Mickey Mouse cupcakes. It was just a great time of celebration. We left September 6, 2015, and I have to say it was amazing. But it was a bittersweet trip and everybody kept saying "You're so lucky you get to go on a cruise that is so awesome! You're so lucky, I wish I was you!" but to be honest we all wish this trip did not exist. Don't get me wrong, we were also excited to experience a Disney cruise and forever grateful to Make-A-Wish for making it happen, but we would've gladly given it up for a chance to erase childhood cancer from our lives. Brian and I would've much rather surprised the girls with a Disney cruise just because.

The whole reason the trip was happening was because Lauren had brain cancer and the truth lingered like a great cloud in the sky. We packed a suitcase full of clothes for each family member, but we also had to pack two extra full suitcases of medical supplies and medications. Make-A-Wish arranged an amazing flight and room for us on the cruise, but they had to be handicap accessible. Lauren told everyone that she had an amazing time, but that she felt like she was squeezing in all the fun she had missed over the last 18 months. Cancer still sucks, even Disney couldn't take that away. Mickey Mouse couldn't wish away or wave away the pain. We went, and we had an absolutely incredible time, but we didn't lose sight of the fight. We didn't lose sight of the need for a cure and the reality of where we were. But what Disney and Make-A-Wish did do was allow Lauren to experience laughter and joy. She got to swim with dolphins and even ride them. I'll never forget sitting next to her that day, looking at her face, and seeing a glimpse of joy without burden. For a moment, her worries were gone.

In October 2015, Lauren got to participate in a special event that raises funds and awareness for childhood cancer. Individuals volunteer to collect donations from friends and family, and when their goal is met they shave their heads. One of Lauren's teachers decided to participate, and convinced the middle school principal to also volunteer. When her principal met his goal, Lauren got to shave her principal's head! He put a chair in the middle rotunda at school and let Lauren shave his head during class change. It's so awesome how her school has rallied around her in support.

Another really cool event that Lauren got to take part in was the Brian McCann Rally Foundation whiffle ball game in November of 2015. Brian McCann used to play for the Atlanta Braves as a catcher, and he was one of Lauren's favorites to watch. He now plays for the Yankees, but still plays a huge role in helping raise awareness and funds with the Rally Foundation to research cures for childhood cancer. Every year, he hosts a softball game with local and national athletes and radio and TV celebrities for the families and kids with cancer. This year, because of the weather, they moved it indoors and had a whiffle ball game instead. The patients got to go up and actually play ball with the celebrities. Lauren was one of the first to go out and give it a try. Brian McCann pitched the ball to her, and she hit a double off of him. Her next time up, she hit a home run.

To watch her swing the bat and walk around the bases with a huge smile on her face and a big, strong athlete holding her hand, cheering her on, was so cool. She was the hero, she was the star, and that's exactly what those kids deserve. It was a really fun event, and I can't say enough about how humble and genuine Brian and Ashley McCann are, and how much they care about these kids and finding a cure.

These were just a few of the incredible opportunities for Lauren and other kids with cancer. We now know that there are many celebrities and organizations who fight to end childhood cancer, and who bring hope and support to families enduring this trial. Events like these help sprinkle happiness among the many tough days that come with childhood cancer, and we were so thankful to experience them.

Lauren, sitting like a princess—foot brace, colorful socks, and all. Even as she received special treatment, she bore the responsibility of raising awareness for all children who have cancer.

CHAPTER 21

"And the God of all grace, who called you to his eternal glory in Christ, after you have suffered a little while, will himself restore you and make you strong, firm and steadfast" 1 Peter 5:10 NIV.

Some people didn't understand why we didn't have a big party when Lauren finished her last chemo treatment in April, but I can guarantee you every cancer mom understood. Although I don't follow a large number of cancer kids, I follow enough stories to know the trend. In this world that we are living in called childhood cancer, it can be foolish to believe that the end of treatment is really the end of your journey. Rather, the end of treatment is often just a stepping stone into the next phase. As another mom so beautifully described it, "You never completely relax because you know that stuff is coming back."

You see, following the stories of other kids means hearing about relapse, new cancers caused by treatment of the first, and often even death. You become so close-knit that their heartbreak becomes your own.

The normal we used to know will never be found again. We live within a new normal now. I want to be honest and real and tell people about the pain because it is so important to acknowledge it. It is important to be honest in saying that tragedy hurts, it hurts bad and if we try to deny it or act like we don't experience it then we are doing ourselves a disservice and fooling ourselves. We won't learn to cope or move past it until we recognize it and admit that it is there. Tragedy hurts, there is pain that seems unbearable, and there are sad parts that can't be fixed. The hurt never completely goes away, but changes over time. Even though chemotherapy and radiation are in the past, the reality of all of the damage done to Lauren's little body keeps us guessing most days. Will she wake up ready to dance and go to school and take on the world, or will she wake up vomiting and in terrible pain, dizzy and confused? Will she continue to keep up with her classmates, or will all of this eventually catch up to her and drag her behind? Will she ever not look like a steroid balloon? Will she be able to jump and run? *When will this be over?!*

The reality is that it probably will never be over. If we are lucky, it will diminish over time, but only time will tell. There is no way to know what is to come. I read about other parents losing their children to pediatric cancer and I think to myself, "Would they gladly trade places with me, to have their baby back, even if it meant never knowing what the next day holds? Even though it meant constantly balancing doctor's appointments, medications, and therapies?" I feel certain the answer is yes, but watching your child suffer is a different kind of misery. Even on the best days, cancer is still lurking, laughing at the marks it's left behind.

For the second year in a row, I was invited to The Quiet Heroes banquet, and I went, this time with a lot fewer hesitations. It was September of 2015, and these events had become more normal for me. I sat next to a mom who I had met at another event. I knew she'd lost her child to cancer several years ago, but she continued to come to cancer community events. On my left

Chapter 21

was a mom who was brand-new, and I was suddenly very aware that I was no longer in the "new" category. I was now the mom who had become so much a part of the cancer community scene that it wasn't a surprise anymore, it wasn't a shock anymore. This was the new normal, and yes the path I've taken is scary, but we're making it one day at a time.

The swag bags were just as amazing as the previous year, but this time I was able to enjoy the company a little bit more, seeing old friends and meeting new ones. I had the opportunity to share words of hope, advice, and encouragement with some moms who were new to the childhood cancer community, the group that none of us want to be a part of. I profoundly sensed that we truly were quiet heroes, what a perfect name for moms of kids with cancer.

But I was also beginning to pull myself out of the childhood cancer community. Since Lauren's treatment had finished, we no longer spent days on end in the hospital. In some weird, strange way you begin to miss those comforting walls and hallways as your journey takes you home more and in the hospital less. Our nurses and practitioners warned us that may people experience a sort of separation anxiety when treatment is over. At the time, I couldn't imagine that to be true, but when we stopped going for scheduled chemotherapy and hospitalizations, I started to understand. CHOA had become home, and our actual home had become a strange place to us. At home, you can't wander the halls in the middle of the night and find another worried mom to chat or have coffee with. You can't ask someone for an extra pillow and warm blanket. You can't look out the window to see the reassuring sight of a team of doctors and nurses whose sole focus is healing your sweet baby. From the quiet, still of a 2:00 AM Saturday morning when the hospital halls are empty, to the hustle and bustle of a Monday 8:00 AM when every doctor is in the house and all of the departments are full with appointments while you're just trying to survive, every day in that place is special. Miracles are happening, angels are walking the halls, and lives are being saved.

You eat there, sleep there, and do your laundry and your hair there. You pay your bills, order takeout, plan your grocery list, and exercise there. You know everyone, from the coffee shop attendant, to the chef, to the housekeepers, and everyone knows you too. When you make friends with the other families who are practically living there, then you become like neighbors. You wonder about each other when one isn't there and you look for each other when you are there. You can sit in the family lounge and ask the other person about the farm and siblings and other details in his life because you know him too well. But now we're no longer as close to the childhood cancer community or the children's hospital community. We're retreating back into our own family and learning how to cherish the small, precious moments.

I remember one day when I washed Lauren's hair. That's it. I washed her hair, like so many moms do every single day, but it was a magical moment. I never thought washing my child's hair, especially at the age of 11, would give me goosebumps. It wasn't even this special when she was a newborn. There are a lot of things I never thought about before I was a mom, or even when my children were young. Everyone gives you advice when you're pregnant, "Oh, cherish each day! They grow up too fast! Time flies!" Nobody says cherish each day because you might not have as many as you expect.

We all know the fact that life is temporary, but it just doesn't seem real to you that your child might leave this world way sooner than you expect. It had been a year and a half since

Chapter 21

our world was rocked by cancer, and considering all she'd been through and the diagnosis she was given, Lauren was doing very well. There are so many parents who have not had that same opportunity to wash hair, so many kids have lost their life to this horrible disease. Maybe that's why I began pulling myself from the cancer community, to separate myself from that pain, at least for a little while.

As I wrote this book in the last months of 2015, Christmas came again, and this time all of our family was together. We were so grateful to all be alive and in the same house, but in 2014 all of our traditions and routines had been shaken to the core. This year, we find ourselves wondering what we should do. Should we buy a tree and put it up, or should we focus our time on just being together? Do we buy tons of presents, or take the kids somewhere fun for an experience instead? There was just something different this year, an overwhelming peace of avoiding the hustle and bustle without guilt, and really just focusing on what the season and holidays are about. Our kids didn't seem to care whether we have a tree or not. They would rather cuddle on the couch all together and watch a Christmas movie. Lauren was just thankful to be out of the hospital, with very little chance of going back in. And as for me, I was just thankful to have all of my kids healthy and in one place.

There's just something about going through a tragedy or major trial like this that changes your perspective on everything. So much of the frivolous part of life just seems so shallow now. All the things that I used to feel like I just had to do because it was Christmastime don't seem that big a deal anymore. If we bake cookies, fine. If we don't, that's okay too. It just kind of rocks you to the core, and there's just something that doesn't seem right about going back to the normal that was normal before cancer.

You can't go back, your life and mind are forever changed.

This year, we knew that we wanted to give back to the community that had so generously provided for us. Lauren wanted to do the same thing she had done the year before, so we designed another shirt to sell. Stepping out in faith, I bought the gifts for her "holiday angel family" before the shirts were sold. After the gifts were bought and the selling deadline passed, we were a bit short. But, true to form, God provided the remainder of the cost in the form of three donors who provided cash gifts to make up the difference.

A week after delivering those gifts, God surprised us with the news that a donor from a different organization had specifically chosen our family to give gifts to this year. I tried to politely decline, explaining that I was sure another family needed it more and that we were okay, but I was assured that the family knew us well and wanted specifically to bless us. Again, God is reminding me to humbly accept His blessings, no matter what form they come in, and allow others to experience giving in a special way. The beautiful cycle of giving and receiving is such a blessed representation of God providing for His people. We help others whenever we can, and others in turn help us. It isn't always an even exchange, in fact it rarely is, but in God's economy, the needs are met and the blessings are abundant.

Perhaps part of what was underneath our Christmas celebration this year was the knowledge that a day that we'd long been anticipating was finally coming. When Lauren had been diagnosed with cancer, the first steps toward treatment were to insert two chemo ports (chest and brain) and a feeding tube. For almost two years, those devices had given her life. It felt so surreal, I had to get to this day before I could really believe it. These two devices provided an avenue for chemotherapy to

Chapter 21

infuse through her entire body for a year, killing cancer cells and providing hope for her future. These two devices provided a means for numerous blood transfusions, IV fluids, electrolytes, and medications to work their magic and save her life. Surgically implanting these two devices was one of the very first steps that had to be taken after her diagnosis of brain cancer, preparing her little body for the biggest fight of her life. They have served her well. But on December 28, 2015, Lauren had surgery to remove these two devices from her body. After 21 months, she was finally free of medical devices.

We went to the hospital that morning and checked in. Lauren was very sleepy, so she slept in the car ride and waiting room. When they called us back into the pre-op room, my friend Kristy came to visit. She and I had worked together in the PICU and she had since transferred to day surgery. She brought Lauren a balloon, devotional, and stuffed animal. She was there when the devices were put in 21 months before, and it was so fitting that God placed her there again on that day. Lauren's nurse came in to go over medical history and medications, then the general surgeon came in to go over his portion. He came, his physician assistant came, and the anesthesiologist came. Lauren's grandparents arrived as well as Brian, and we all kept Lauren entertained while waiting. Then, the nurse came and said it was time for her sleepy medicine. I asked where the neurosurgeon was, and she said he'd be in soon. He was the first physician to become a part of Lauren's journey, he removed her brain tumor, preserving her brain and saving her life. He became a source of great security and hope for us in her journey. I felt as though I couldn't rest until I saw him and had his reassurance.

Lauren began to get silly and eventually dozed off. About an hour later, the nurse said it was time to go. We all kissed her goodbye and they wheeled her away. I told the nurse that I still hadn't seen the neurosurgeon. She said he was finishing another case and would come see me afterwards. I just couldn't settle until I saw him. He was there for her on day one and he had a significant role in saving her life. I have such a sense of security when he is around. I know he cares for Lauren.

After several more minutes, he came and went over his portion of the procedure and told us Lauren would need to spend the night. We had anticipated this, so we weren't surprised. We spent the next hour and a half waiting. I tried to stay distracted by chatting with my parents and in-laws, but deep in my heart I was wanting so badly for surgery to be over. I needed this part to be done. Putting this behind us would be a huge milestone, the closing of a chapter.

We have learned not to get too comfortable and say that our journey is over. Childhood cancer leaves a path of destruction whose remnants linger for life. But that day we made a huge step forward, closing another chapter, and we are so thankful to God for getting us this far. The physical freedom from medical devices provided us a sense of mental freedom, of breaking the shackles and telling cancer that enough was enough. We won.

AFTERWARD

"For God has not given us a spirit of fear, but of power and of love and of a sound mind" 2 Timothy 1:7. NKJV

Throughout this journey through childhood cancer, so many things were uncertain. Questions of fear and doubt would run through my mind. Would Lauren live through treatment? Would her cancer return? Would she be neurologically devastated by brain surgery and treatment? Would the treatments cause terrible side effects? Would my other two girls rebel or become depressed? Would Brian and I grow apart? Would we be able to maintain our jobs, our home, and our financial obligations? Would we have to borrow money? Would my new boss be supportive? Would Lauren fall behind in school? Would the treatment work? How much time would we spend in the hospital? What days would we be in the hospital? How would we handle holidays? Could we commit to any events? Would we make it through the night in our own beds?

Every day was a new adventure, never knowing if a twist or turn was up ahead. Would Lauren eat or not? Would she be in pain or strong enough to play? Would we ever feel normal again? The eternal vision was secure, but the day to day elements were always uncertain. Audrey and Haley would never know who would be home after school, or if we'd all be in the hospital. And later in the journey, we sometimes did not know how everyone was going to get to school, work, and appointments because of all the variables. The uncertainty remains to some degree. Will she relapse? Will she have health complications later in life? Will she be able to readjust socially? Will we ever feel like we are through this journey? Will it ever be behind us? Who knows?

God knows. His security trumps our fleshly uncertainties. That's where underlying peace comes from. Not in removing the uncertainties of what will play out, but by covering them in the blanket of security that God's will wins and all will be made right—somehow.

Yet, when I think of Lauren's cancer journey, the word "secure" stands out. Although there were great bits of uncertainty, there was an equal amount of security. Security in having CHOA for treatment. Security in knowing the doctors, nurses, and workings of the hospital. Knowing that finances wouldn't likely be a huge factor with our two good jobs, our neighbors and friends, two sets of grandparents, and three insurances. I also felt great security in my family unit. My girls were close and strong, Brian was—and is—a rock for all of us, totally committed to us for life, no matter what. I felt security in the support of my job. Most importantly, I felt security from God. Regardless of the path or outcome, God was in control and He would work it out for good. I never doubted that. My hope was secure, in Christ's promises. Secure. Yes, her treatment was secure, her chances were as secure as possible for survival, and our resources were secure. My family and our support system was secure. And our heavenly Father was secure, more secure than any earthly disease could counter. That sense of security provides comfort, peace, confidence, reassurance, hope, help, and love. Security provides an underlying sense that everything will be ok despite the seemingly chaotic surrounding and circumstances. Security says, "This will come to an end and peace will be restored." Security says, "In the end, it will all be ok." Security allows you to weather storms, balance unsteady bridges, and walk through darkness, knowing that help and hope are on the other side.

God is security. God is our hope, help, peace, and reassurance. My hope is secure in Christ! I love that security. I love that reassurance for it allows me to never feel helpless or hopeless even in what seem like the worst circumstances imaginable. In fact, this security is exactly what I want to convey through my "Anchors 4 Hope" ministry. I want everyone I encounter to experience this security personally. I want everyone to know without a shadow of a doubt that everything will be ok in the end, because of our hope in Christ. That is the ultimate message. Jesus' death on the cross is our eternal security. Even in the face of death, we can fear no evil. "Death, where is your sting?" There is no fear when we have eternal security, eternal hope.

In watching Lauren battle with childhood cancer, which is far from over, we have been so glad to serve a God who promised to give us endurance. Hebrews 12:1 says, "Since we are surrounded by so great a cloud of witnesses let us lay aside everything that hinders and the sin that so easily ensnares us and let us run with endurance the race that is set before us." Every single person in our lives at that time was a part of the cloud of witnesses. Every cancer family we met, every friend, neighbor, and family member, every volunteer, and so many of the organizations were all encouragers. We were so thankful because of them. Because of God's grace and mercy we were able to set the heavy weight called cancer aside and we could cast away the sin of anger and doubt.

Anchors for Hope

We could run. Run! God promised a victorious finish line and regardless of how our race played out on earth our heavenly finish line would be a guaranteed Glory Land.

We all are running a race of some kind. Yours may not be cancer. It may be something totally different. It may be some other illness or addiction. You may be struggling with divorce or loneliness, depression or anxiety, or maybe you were just running the rat race in everyday life . . . get the kids up, feed the kids, off to school, go to work, clean house, run errands, grocery shop, pay the bills, pick up the kids, feed the kids, shuttle them to a multitude of activities, homework, chores, laundry, dishes, and finally off to bed. Then you wake up the next morning and repeat. And somewhere in all of those races you had to find time for yourself and your spouse. But there is an answer for all these races, an endurance source that will propel you joyfully to the end. All you have to do is seek Him. God is your answer. He is there when you're sick and tired and depressed. He can handle your anger, and He will gently console you. He will guide you through that rat race and give you wisdom as to which activities glorify Him and which should go. He will give you peace. He will give you hope and energy and joy. I'm telling you as someone who learned this the hard way too many times, and as one who is finally getting it as I watch my child fight for her life: God has ultimate control, and if we willingly humble ourselves and submit to His control, the joy and peace we find is overwhelming. There is no race too tough for God's endurance.

Even as I wrote in my own journal, God put this lesson right in front of my face again. When I sat down to write one day, Lauren was sleeping, exhausted just from sitting up on the couch for a few hours. I poured out my concern over Lauren's decreased endurance and ranted about trusting God to provide

Afterward

it. Then I watched him work. As I wrapped up my entry, sitting across the table from me was that same girl, who now had her nose in the books doing homework so that she wouldn't fall behind her classmates. He was providing her the endurance, in that very moment. God is good all the time. Don't simply take my word for it. You can find out for yourself, and I promise that you will not be disappointed.

In the process of this journey, I was reminded that God was with us. There were days when His message was so strong that I couldn't help but shout it out. Then there were days when His presence was equally strong, but His message was simply the quiet whisper of comfort in my ears. Encouragement from friends, the warmth of the sun on our skin, so many small things reminded us that God cares for us and loves us. When Lauren was diagnosed with a brain tumor on March 11, 2014, I told God I did not need to know why. I only needed to know "what." What did He want to accomplish through us in this journey? What did He want us to do? Lauren had made it clear that she wanted to share hope and joy with everyone she met along the way and what better way to share God's love than to tell about the miracles He was working in our lives?

If you did not know Him, or if you have lost the sense of His peace in your own life, I hope you seek Him now. The hope and joy that He provides through salvation is more than any earthly substitute can ever come close to matching. My prayer is that everyone who reads this book and does not have a personal relationship with Jesus Christ will develop a desire for Him and accept Him. For anyone who reads this book and already has that relationship, my prayer is that you somehow are able to grow to increase your hope and joy through Lauren's story. I know I sure have. I know for sure that God is blessed by the love and cheerful giving so many have shown to us.

ABOUT THE AUTHOR

Karen Furr lives outside of Atlanta, Georgia with her husband, two daughters, stepdaughter, and dog named Hope. She writes and speaks about learning to lean on Christ during times of crisis. Her world was thrown into a tailspin when her youngest daughter, Lauren, was diagnosed with a rare form of brain cancer at the age of nine. She struggled to continue on as a wife, mom, stepmom, daughter, sister, and nurse, even as she desperately watched her little girl battle cancer. Karen learned that the only way through was to rely on Christ as her anchor for hope during the storm of childhood cancer. Now, Lauren is in remission, and Karen shares Lauren's story, God's word, and how to find hope in Christ during life's storms.

Karen invites you to join the community of people leaning on Christ during life's storms at **www.anchors4hope.com**.

Videos of Lauren's cancer journey

- "I Like Bald Heads" music video
  http://anchorsforhope.com/baldheads

- Atlanta Hawks experience video
  http://anchorsforhope.com/Hawks

- "Oh The Places They'll Go" video
  http://anchorsforhope.com/places

Websites of childhood cancer

www.curechildhoodcancer.org

www.rallyfoundation.org

www.teamsummer.org

www.wish.org

www.thetruth365.org

www.choa.org

www.stepupbeavoice.com

Credits

Thank you to Allison Crews Photography for the beautiful photos of Lauren and to Anointing Productions for the gorgeous cover design and formatting of this book.

Thank you for buying my book!

I'd like to offer you a FREE GIFT:

15 Practical Ways to Help a Family In Need (Besides a Casserole!)

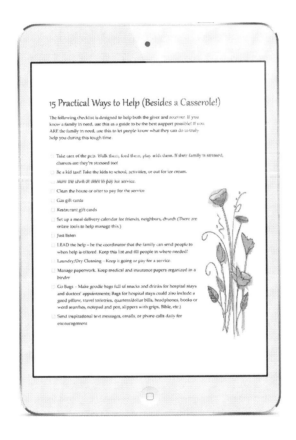

Grab your copy FREE at
AnchorsForHope.com/FreeGift

Made in the USA
Lexington, KY
04 April 2016